The Stylish Girl's Guide to fabulous Cocktails

The Stylish Girl's Guide to fabulous Cocktails

Colleen Mullaney

sixth&spring books

contents

4

sixth&spring  books

161 Avenue of the Americas, Suite 1301
New York, New York 10013
sixthandspringbooks.com

Managing Editor WENDY WILLIAMS
Senior Editor MICHELLE BREDESON
Art Director DIANE LAMPHRON
Assistant Designer SARAH DEVITA
Illustrations BEE (larkworthy.com)
Editor ANNIE LEAH SOMMERS
Copy Editor KRISTINA SIGLER

Vice President, Publisher TRISHA MALCOLM
Creative Director JOE VIOR
Production Manager DAVID JOINNIDES
President ART JOINNIDES

Library of Congress Control Number:
2009943426
ISBN: 978-1-933027-96-8
Manufactured in China
1 3 5 7 9 10 8 6 4 2
First Edition

5

cocktails are the new black

Cocktails are the trend du jour. They're hotter than hot. And like the latest designer shoes, the more you want them, the more expensive they get. But why limit yourself to the offerings at the bar when you can make one yourself to suit your every mood, every occasion, every outfit? Get ready to mix and match—literally.

In my previous cocktail book, *It's 5 o'clock Somewhere*, I took readers on a world tour of cocktails, focusing on drinks inspired by my favorite international cities and global hotspots. In this book, I set out to do something a little different: to create and share drink recipes that every stylish girl should have in her cocktail wardrobe. Whether you're hosting a special event, having a romantic evening for two or mixing up a batch of drinks for "girls' night in," you'll find the ideal libation to do so in style.

Each chapter in this guide focuses on a different spirit and its unique characteristics. We all know that different shoes have distinctive personalities. You have your flats that make you feel grounded, boots that give you attitude and heels that give you a lift. In much the same way, each spirit has its own personality. Gin is the classic confidence-builder, like those black patent-leather pumps and gold bangles.

Champagne is celebratory. It's the evening gown of the cocktail world. And wine is like a great pair of jeans that will see you through any occasion with style to spare.

I've included more than eighty of my favorite cocktails—ones that I've created through countless hours of sipping and mixing (I hope you appreciate my sacrifice), as well as a few timeless classics. With each recipe I make my suggestion of which shoes best reflect the spirit of the cocktail. It's up to you to decide which comes first, the shoes or the cocktail. Look for the entertaining and shopping tips, guides to matching cocktails with your favorite movies or fashion personality and even a cocktail horoscope! Finally, in "Accessories" you'll find cocktail bar lingo, downloadable playlists and more.

In the end you'll see that all go together. Life, cocktails, style...but not necessarily in that order.

note

None of these cocktails should be drunk while donning a robe and slippers. (Unless of course the robe is silk and you have a pair of to-die-for heels on.) I also discourage drinking alone, so all the recipes are for four. Besides, who would you share all that style with?

cocktail bar must-haves

If you're going to put together a superb cocktail, you have to have the right tools. After all, it's not very stylish to serve your guests out of a plastic punch bowl and Dixie cups.

Barware

Invest in a few essential tools to ensure your cocktails will be delicious *and* chic.

- Glass pitcher
- Shaker—metal or glass with a strainer top
- Bottle opener
- Citrus juicer
- Muddler
- Bar towels
- Ice bucket
- Ice tongs
- Ice cube trays
- Picks
- Stirrers
- Straws
- Coasters
- Cocktail napkins
- Blender for frozen drinks

Spirits

Since you will be mixing them with other ingredients you don't have to buy top-of-the-line spirits, but buy good quality.

gin
rum (white)
tequila blanco
brandy

vodka
straight or flavored (citrus is a good basic choice)

liqueurs
such as Cointreau, limoncello, Godiva Milk Chocolate liqueur, Tuaca and St-Germain

white wine
a variety, such as chardonnay, pinot grigio and sauvignon blanc

red wine
a variety, such as cabernet, pinot noir and Chianti

champagne
brut and/or rosé

prosecco
a sparkling white wine similar to champagne

Glasses

**The glasses you use to serve the cocktails set the tone.
Here are a few you can't live without.**

White wine
glasses

Red wine
goblets

Champagne
flutes

Martini glasses

Hurricane
glasses

Highball or Collins
glasses

Lowball/rocks
glasses

Mini glasses

Margarita
glasses

Garnishes and Extras
Every cocktail needs the right accessories.

- Lemons
- Limes
- Other fresh fruit, such as oranges, strawberries and pineapple

- Superfine sugar
- Dark or semisweet chocolate bars for shaving
- Fruit juices, such as pomegranate and pineapple

- Olives
- Cocktail onions
- Maraschino cherries
- Mint leaves
- Coarse salt

The Bombed Girl
Gimlet

Martini Classico
Ruby Slipper

The Cover-up
The Slicker

vodka

Sweater Girl
Chocolate
Cashmere
Wrap

Prêt-à-Party
Lemon Drop

Handsome Devil
Morning Glory

Bloody Mary
Fuzzy Navel
Cosmopolitan

Pink Flamingo
Love on the
Line

vodka cocktails

We begin with vodka because it scores very high on mixability and is probably the spirit you have the most of in your cabinet. And it goes well with just about anything (except maybe balsamic vinegar). I think of vodka as a fine lady who is always polished and doesn't need accessories but nevertheless wears them well.

Vodka is the most sophisticated of the spirits—a superb choice for a woman of style. It's a little nostalgic, a tad old Hollywood, a bit Audrey Hepburn in *Breakfast at Tiffany's*. Her character lived with only with a few worldly goods, but always the best. (Who needs a sofa when there are alligator flats to be had?) Not to mention she threw awesome parties. With a bottle of fine vodka, you don't need much else to be eternally in vogue.

Vodka is the most popular spirit, and it's easy to see why. Its smooth flavor mixes unbelievably well with any number of other spirits, liqueurs, fruits and fruit juices. It goes with everything.

Vodka can take you from morning till night. Try a batch of Bloody Marys for brunch, a Martini Classico at lunch and a Cosmopolitan to sip with your girlfriends before, after or instead of a night on the town.

A native of cold climes, vodka will not only warm you up in the winter (try a Chocolate Cashmere Wrap) but also makes smashing cocktails for any time of year (go for a refreshingly luscious Cover-up in beach weather).

When you have the right little black dress, you don't need much else. Likewise, Vodka doesn't need much accessorizing either—just a couple of cubes and a splash. When you drink vodka you don't have to talk much; it speaks volumes for you. Vodka allows you to say something without saying anything at all.

 vodka is a perfect match for that little black dress, red lipstick, pearls and kitten heels.

Martini Classico

SERVES 4

Every stylish girl needs to know how to make a great martini. For a kick, use citrus or fruit-infused vodka. For a fiery finish, try chili pepper vodka and jalepeño-stuffed olives.

2 cups ice
8 oz. (237ml) vodka
2 oz. (59ml) vermouth
Olives for garnish

● Fill a pitcher with ice. Add vodka and vermouth, then stir. Allow flavors to marry for a few minutes. Strain mixture into martini glasses, garnish with olives and serve.

13

Shoes
Match this classic with black patent-leather heels—and pearls, of course!

vodka cocktails

Ruby Slipper
SERVES 4

This is an ideal cocktail for a gathering of girlfriends. Who needs a book club? Make a batch of these and start a shoe club.

8 oz. (237ml) vodka

4 oz. (118ml) triple sec

4 oz. (118ml) pomegranate juice

2 oz. (59ml) freshly squeezed lime juice

1 cup ice

● Mix first four ingredients in a cocktail shaker filled with ice. Allow the mixture to sit for 1 minute, giving time for the flavors to marry. Strain into martini glasses and serve.

shoes
Ruby-colored skimmers are comfortable and chic—no bedroom slippers, please!

14

shoes
Dress like a Bond girl in killer boots with stiletto heels.

The Bombed Girl
SERVES 4

Who doesn't get excited by a gorgeous man in a tux who packs a gun, drives fast cars and has a house account wherever he stays from Paris to Montenegro? I whipped up a batch of these delectable cocktails before my girlfriends and I went to see the latest flick starring the delicious Mr. Bond.

8 oz. (237ml) vodka
4 oz. (118ml) pineapple juice
2 oz. (59ml) white cranberry juice
1 cup ice
4 lemon slices for garnish

● Mix vodka, pineapple juice and white cranberry juice in a cocktail shaker filled with ice. Strain into martini glasses, add lemon slices for garnish and serve.

stylish entertaining

If you're going to be mixing up all these delicious drinks, you owe it to your friends to share. What better way than to throw a party? Here are a few pointers to help make your fête the event of the season!

CHOOSE A THEME.

Bridal shower? Girls' Poker Night? Jane Austen Appreciation Club meeting? The excuse for the soiree (not that you need an excuse) will dictate every element of the party.

SEND OUT INVITATIONS.

Tailor your invites to the event. For a more formal occasion, like a bridal shower, take the time to mail paper invitations. For a more casual affair like Movie Night (see suggestions for stylish flicks on page 94), try Evite.com.

PICK A SIGNATURE COCKTAIL

and mix up a batch. Choose something easy to serve that matches the mood of your gathering. This will add personality to the party and get everyone in the right spirit.

WHIP UP SOME NIBBLES.

Put out a variety of snacks in pretty bowls—everything looks better in silver! Try cheese-flavored popcorn, spicy nuts or fancy chips. Or pick up a variety of cheeses and crackers and arrange them on a stylish serving tray.

FASHION SOME FLOWER POWER.

Bunches of flowers from the local market make a great statement. Cut the stems short and mound the blooms. Carnations, roses, and hydrangea are all excellent choices. Set them around your space for bursts of color.

LIGHT UP THE NIGHT.

There is nothing more glamorous than basking in lush candlelight all evening! Pillars encased in glass hurricanes are great for busy spots like the bar; votives scattered everywhere else will impart a warm, memorable glow.

TURN ON THE TUNES.

Check out the downloadable playlist on page 138 for lots tunes to sip by. They'll help you set the tone for your party, whether you're hosting a tranquil talkfest or full-on living room disco.

WEAR SOMETHING FABULOUS.

You're the hostess after all. Slip into something that fits the theme—and make sure it's comfortable! Finish with snazzy shoes and fashion-forward jewelry and you're ready to shine.

Gimlet
SERVES 4

This is the stylish girl's version of the
house specialty at the Ivy at the Shore
restaurant in Santa Monica, California.
Mix up a batch of these concoctions
while dishing on all the hot gossip.

8 oz. (237ml) vodka

1 cup (237) fresh mint leaves, plus
4 more leaves for garnish

Juice of 2 limes, freshly squeezed

4 lime slices for garnish

2 cups ice

● Pour vodka into a cocktail shaker.
Wash and dry the mint leaves, place in
the shaker and muddle with the vodka for
a few minutes. Squeeze the juice from
the limes into the cocktail shaker and mix.
Allow the flavors to marry for a few
minutes. Using a strainer, pour the mixture
into ice-filled rocks glasses. Garnish
with fresh mint and limes.

17

vodka cocktails

The Cover-up
SERVES 4

Here's après-swim perfection, especially if you moved the party from the beach back to your place for cocktails. You're sure to be the hostess of the moment in your fashionable cover-up and sandals. Music playing, drinks made, party on!

8 oz. (237ml) Absolut Citron vodka

2 oz. (59ml) St-Germain liqueur

3 cups (711ml) watermelon, cubed

2 tablespoons (30ml) key lime juice

1 cup ice

4 straws

Shoes
Metallic sandals that show off your sun-tanned legs and pretty polished toes.

● Put all ingredients into a blender. Blend until the mixture is smooth, about 1 minute. Pour into highball glasses, add straws and serve.

The Slicker

SERVES 4

Like the always fashionable belted trench, these will put a spring in your step and warm you right up on those wet spring days. While the lemon gives a sunny lift, the basil adds a bit of garden spice. Pick up a fresh bunch at the market.

8 oz. (237ml) vodka

8 basil leaves, plus 4 sprigs for garnish

4 oz. (118ml) limoncello

2 oz. (59ml) freshly squeezed lemon juice

1 cup ice

● In a cocktail shaker, muddle the basil leaves with the vodka. Add limoncello and lemon juice. Fill the shaker with ice and shake well. Strain into martini glasses. Garnish each glass with a sprig of basil and serve.

19

Vodka cocktails are perfect any time of year, or any time of day. Vodka's superior mixability can take you right through all of the seasons—in high style.

vodka cocktails

Sweater Girl
SERVES 4

The beginning of autumn is always refreshing. So much to look forward to, so much shopping to do! I make batches of these after football and soccer games when there's a chill in the afternoon air and a sweater is required. The vanilla vodka warms everyone up in a snap.

8 oz. (237ml) Absolut Vanilia vodka

2 oz. (59ml) Tuaca liqueur

4 oz. (118ml) fresh apple cider

4 cups ice—1 for shaker, 3 for glasses

2 oz. (59ml) ginger ale

4 thin apple slices for garnish

shoes
Riding boots—
they have
attitude and
kick.

● Mix the first three ingredients in a cocktail shaker filled with ice. Strain into ice-filled highball glasses and top with ginger ale. Garnish with apple slices and serve.

Chocolate Cashmere Wrap
SERVES 4

The chocolate adds a velvety sweetness while the sugar gives a touch of sparkle— just what a stylish girl needs on a chilly winter evening!

8 oz. (237ml) Absolut Vanilia vodka
4 oz. (118ml) Kahlúa
2 oz. (59ml) Godiva Milk Chocolate liqueur
1 cup ice
Lemon wedge for rimming
Raw sugar for the rims of the glasses
Grated semisweet chocolate shavings for garnish

● Mix vodka, Kahlúa, and Godiva liqueur in a cocktail shaker filled with ice. Rub martini glass rims lightly with lemon wedge. Dip the rims into a shallow dish filled with sugar. Strain the cocktail mixture into the glasses and garnish with chocolate shavings.

shoes
Cozy suede boots.

a shot of style

I prefer to sip a full-size cocktail, but some situations really call for a shot. These mini cocktails are just the thing to jumpstart an evening of bar-hopping. And when you run into your ex arm-in-arm with a lingerie model, a shot really hits the spot.

Prêt-à-Party
SERVES 4

These fruity, shot-size treats give you courage—courage to let the boy know you are available, available to talk to, look at and to kiss.

4 oz. (118ml) vodka
2 oz. (59ml) triple sec
2 oz. (59ml) cranberry juice
1 cup ice

● Mix all ingredients in a cocktail shaker filled with ice. Pour evenly into mini glasses and serve.

shoes
Flats if he's shorter, heels if he's taller.

vodka cocktails

Lemon Drop
SERVES 4

A bit of lemon in this delicious mini cocktail adds some zip to kick off the celebration, the dinner or the reunion. Make a batch and watch your friends pucker up!

6 oz. (177ml) vodka

2 oz. (59ml) limoncello

2 teaspoons (10ml) simple syrup*

1 cup ice

shoes
Strappy gold sandals with something to say.

● Mix all ingredients in a cocktail shaker filled with ice. Pour evenly into mini glasses and serve.

*recipe on page 134

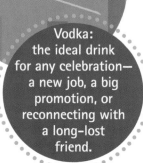

Vodka: the ideal drink for any celebration— a new job, a big promotion, or reconnecting with a long-lost friend.

Handsome Devil
SERVES 4

Volunteered to host the office party?
Just mix up a batch of these cocktails,
put on some party music and see
who hooks up with that handsome
devil from sales...

1 cup ice
8 oz. (237ml) vodka
8 oz. (237ml) pineapple juice
4 oz. (118ml) hibiscus liqueur
2 oz. (59ml) lime juice
4 lime slices for garnish.

● Pour all ingredients into a large
shaker half-filled with ice. Shake.
Strain into martini glasses, garnish
with lime slices and serve.

25

Shoes:
High-heeled
Mary Janes are
office and party
appropriate.

Morning Glory
SERVES 4

I love to have friends over on a lazy weekend morning, whip up a pitcher of Morning Glories and watch the morning melt into the afternoon! My brunches have gone into late afternoon hours on more than one occasion. Add a potato-and-onion frittata, roasted asparagus and fruit salad and off you go.

8 oz. (237ml) Absolut Mandrin vodka
8 oz. (237ml) tangerine juice
4 oz. (118ml) mango nectar
Juice of 1 lemon, freshly squeezed
2 cups ice
4 lemon slices for garnish

● Mix vodka, tangerine juice, mango nectar and lemon juice in a cocktail shaker. Pour mixture into ice-filled rocks glasses. Garnish with lemon slices and serve.

26

Vodka accessorizes well with all kinds of fruits and fruit juices, from limes to mangoes to blackberries.

Shoes
Ballet flats with a bit of glam take you from cooking to brunching.

Bloody Mary

SERVES 4

This classic brunch beverage is both piquant and refreshing, and the lime juice adds extra citrus while calming the spicy flavors a bit. Leave a bottle of hot sauce next to the pitcher for those who want to dial things up.

32 oz. (946ml) tomato juice

8 oz. (237ml) vodka

2 oz. (59ml) freshly squeezed lime juice

2 tablespoons (30ml) freshly squeezed lemon juice

2 tablespoons (30ml) prepared horseradish

2 tablespoons (30ml) Worcestershire sauce

1 teaspoon (5ml) hot pepper sauce

1 teaspoon (5ml) celery salt

1 teaspoon (5ml) freshly ground black pepper

3 cups ice

4 celery stalks for garnish

4 lemon wedges and 4 lime wedges for garnish

4 wooden skewers

● In a large pitcher, mix together all ingredients. Pour into ice-filled highball glasses. Garnish with skewered lemon and lime wedges and small celery stalks.

Shoes
Animal prints—flats for recharging after a late night, heels for brunching and getting the day under way.

vodka cocktails

Fuzzy Navel
SERVES 4

Serve this versatile cocktail in a martini glass for an evening drink or go heavier on the orange juice and use tall glasses for a delightful brunch addition. Substituting ruby-red grapefruit juice for the orange juice will add fruity fabulousness.

8 oz. (237ml) Absolut Apeach vodka
4 oz. (118ml) peach schnapps
8 oz. (237ml) freshly squeezed orange juice
1 cup ice
4 orange slices for garnish

● Mix all ingredients in a cocktail shaker filled with ice. Strain into lowball glasses. Garnish with slices of orange and serve.

shoes
In satin D'Orsay heels, you'll shine as bright as this vivacious cocktail.

Cosmopolitan
SERVES 4

Shoes
Peacock-blue
jeweled pumps
á la Carrie
Bradshaw.

A Cosmo will lift any mood. If you have cranky feelings after enjoying one of these, have another—two might just balance those hormones right out. I'm very into balance. I am a Libra, after all.

29

8 oz. (237ml) vodka
4 oz. (118ml) triple sec
2 oz. (59ml) freshly squeezed lime juice
2 oz. (59ml) cranberry juice
1 cup ice
4 lime slices for garnish

● Mix all ingredients in a shaker filled with ice. Strain into martini glasses. Garnish with lime slices and serve.

vodka cocktails

Pink Flamingo
SERVES 4

I made these pink beauties for a fête in honor of a girlfriend who was visiting from Australia, and let me tell you, they flew. I was dressed to match in a bright pink minidress. I did up the table with bright pink and orange dahlia blossoms, limes and lemongrass in glass cubes filled with water and floating candles, and votives in orange and yellow glass globes. It was a magical fun- and friend-filled evening.

shoes
Strappy gold sandals with something to say.

8 oz. (237ml) Absolut Ruby Red vodka

4 oz. (118ml) ruby-red grapefruit juice

2 oz. (59ml) passion-fruit nectar

Juice of 1 lime, freshly squeezed

3 cups ice—1 cup for shaker, 2 for glasses

4 oz. (118ml) Prosecco

4 lime slices for garnish

● In a large cocktail shaker filled with ice, mix together the first four ingredients. Shake well. Strain into ice-filled Collins glasses and top off with Prosecco. Garnish with lime slices and serve.

Love on the Line
SERVES 4

Vodka is what you drink when have no idea how on earth you are going to find someone new to love and to love you, and then you do! Because you are a fabulous you!

8 oz. (237ml) Absolut Raspberri vodka

2 oz. (59ml) limoncello

4 oz. (118ml) berry juice (blackberry, raspberry, or mix of)

3 cups ice—1 cup for shaker, 2 for glasses.

Seltzer to top

4 mint sprigs for garnish

● Mix vodka, limoncello and berry juice in a cocktail shaker filled with ice. Strain into ice-filled rocks glasses, then top with seltzer. Garnish with mint sprigs and serve.

Shoes
Before the love,
snakeskin heels,
after the love,
bare feet!

Already Gone
Limetini

Gibson Martini
Royal Flush

gin

Martini Classico
Tina Collins

The Confession
The Madison

Coco's Pearls
Gin Press

CLASSIC CHIC

gin drinks

Gin is the classic go-to libation. Need something to kick off the dinner party with the boss? Whip up a Gibson Martini. Girlfriends on their way over for the meeting of your book, knitting or poker club? Try a Royal Flush. You can never go wrong. Like a Kelly bag, a navy blue cashmere sweater or ballet flats, gin is iconic.

Gin is a little bit retro, like the Tom Collins (try my Tina Collins—who needs a man when you have gin?), but always up-to-date, like the lime and mint deliciousness of a Limetini.

The woman who drinks gin is sure of herself and her style. Never showy, she doesn't have to make a scene to get noticed. She knows it's far sexier to slip into a room unannounced, and then have the room notice her.

Gin gives you strength to overlook—or not look too closely at—the wrinkles, laugh lines and fine lines, expanding hips or sagging boobs, but it gives you the courage to look at what they brought you: years of laughter, hard-earned wisdom, children, carrying on when you

thought you might not and carrying others when they needed you to.

For better or for worse, gin gives you the courage to confess things, things you normally would stay far away from—things you thought you would never tell anyone in a million years.

Gin gives you courage to do something you've never done before but always wanted to: take tango lessons, learn Italian, belly dance, go to the movies alone, be a better friend, wear that lace negligee set that's been in your drawer for a year. Travel somewhere, anywhere. (I keep my passport at the ready just in case. I love to go places. I'll go anywhere, anytime, as long as there's beauty to look at and cocktails to be had.)

Gin gives you the courage to say "I'm fabulous," and mean it.

Gibson Martini
SERVES 4

This classic cocktail is timeless and back in fashion. Try a splash of citrus or fruit juice for a sweet infusion.

6 oz. (177ml) gin, well-chilled

2 oz. (59ml) vermouth

1 cup ice

4 pickled onions for garnish

Cocktail picks

● Mix gin and vermouth in a cocktail shaker filled with ice. Strain into martini glasses. Garnish with skewered onions on cocktail picks. Serve.

shoes
Red patent-leather pumps are always in style.

gin drinks

Royal Flush
SERVES 4

Gin makes the ideal girls'-night-in cocktail. It goes well with books, movies, beading, knitting and facials. And it's especially good for Girls' Poker Night! It gets interesting when instead of chips, the girls throw in items from their closets! I have won a few fabulous and frilly items! Serve these cocktails with spicy nuts, Parmesan popcorn and cheese puffs.

8 oz. (237ml) gin

4 oz. (118ml) maraschino liqueur

4 oz. (118ml) Cointreau

2 oz. (59ml) grenadine

2 tablespoons (30ml) freshly squeezed lime juice

8 oz. (237ml) pineapple juice

Dash of bitters

3 cups ice

4 cherries for garnish

shoes
Vintage peep-toes will keep you on your toes!

● Pour ingredients into a large pitcher and mix well. Pour mixture into ice-filled highball glasses. Garnish with cherries and serve.

Already Gone
SERVES 4

Shoes
Wedges—you need to be grounded when making big decisions.

Perfect for drinking while you decide whether he should go, or you should. To take it up a notch, substitute cherry brandy for the grenadine.

8 oz. (237ml) gin

2 oz. (59ml) freshly squeezed lemon juice

2 oz. (59ml) grenadine

2 tablespoons (30ml) simple syrup*

2 cups ice

Club soda to top

4 orange slices for garnish

● Mix first four ingredients in a large pitcher filled with ice. Let sit for a few minutes so the mixture chills and the flavors marry. Strain into martini glasses, top off with club soda, garnish with orange slices and serve.

*recipe on page 134

37

Limetini
SERVES 4

Mint and lime are a match made in heaven, especially when plunged into gin. It's the just-right cocktail for cooling your taste buds when things get too hot.

8 mint leaves
2 oz. (59ml) simple syrup*
2 oz. (59ml) freshly squeezed lime juice
8 oz. (237ml) gin
1 cup ice

● Muddle the mint with the simple syrup and fresh lime juice in shaker. Let sit for a few minutes and allow the flavors to marry. Add gin and ice and shake well. Strain into martini glasses serve.

*recipe on page 134

shoes
Chic sneaks—Pumas or Converse. No brown tree-hugger shoes— we are stylish, need I remind you.

Shoes
Slingback heels
will stay on in case
you need to make
a quick exit.

The Confession

SERVES 4

I have heard many confessions while enjoying gin. They usually start out with "You know, I haven't really told anyone this before, but...." At this point you really need to stop and say, "Let me pour you another drink."

8 oz. (237ml) gin

2 oz. (59ml) limoncello

2 oz. (59ml) peach juice or nectar

2 oz. (59ml) raspberry juice

2 cups ice

12 fresh raspberries for garnish

● Combine all liquid ingredients in a cocktail shaker and mix well. Pour into ice-filled rocks glasses. Garnish with fresh raspberries and serve.

Gin is excellent for the après-power shop. After hitting the stores with the girls, mix cocktails and show off your finds.

gin drinks

The Madison
SERVES 4

I have mixed up these cocktails after many successful shopping days sauntering around New York, from downtown and SoHo up to Fifth Avenue and Madison. But when you're with friends, it doesn't matter where you shop—just that you do!

8 oz. (237ml) gin

4 oz. (118ml) peach brandy

4 oz. (118ml) pomegranate juice

2 oz. (59ml) tangerine juice

1 cup ice

4 orange slices for garnish

Shoes
Something with low heels—one must always shop with style, but be practical, as you'll be walking all day.

● Mix all liquid ingredients in a cocktail shaker filled with ice. Strain into martini glasses, garnish with orange slices and serve.

power-shopping pointers

Sure, you've been shopping since before you could pronounce Manolo Blahnik, but there may be a trick or two even you haven't thought of!

MAKE A LIST OF KEY ITEMS YOU'RE LOOKING FOR.
A list and a plan ensure that you will be focused and avoid buying more tops when you're actually on a mad search for skirts!

SAVVY SHOPPERS HAVE A BUDGET.
Make smart choices, but if there is an incredible sale on that charcoal-gray cashmere sweater you've been eyeing, well...need I say more?

WEAR AN OUTFIT THAT'S EASY TO SLIP ON AND OFF.
It saves time and lets you shimmy into that divine cocktail dress in a snap! There's nothing more tiring when you're shopping than fighting your way through layers of clothing or wrestling with tons of buttons or snaps.

CARRY A LIGHTWEIGHT SHOULDER BAG THAT KEEPS YOUR HANDS FREE.
All the better to work the racks or flit around the shops and sample the merchandise.

BRING A SMALL NOTEBOOK FOR JOTTING DOWN IDEAS OR TAKE SNAPS WITH YOUR CAMERA PHONE.
It will help you keep track of trends or remember the gorgeous ensemble that mannequin was wearing.

LEAVE THE STILETTOS OR HIGH-HEELED BOOTS AT HOME.
Comfort is key during a power shop. Try wedges—comfort with a heel!

BRING A FRIEND.
Not only is it more fun to shop with a friend (and who else are you going to have cocktails with after?), a friend can also help you pinpoint what looks good and what is best left on the rack.

FUEL UP FOR A POWER-FILLED POWER SHOP!
Have lunch first or bring a snack (but leave the cocktails for after!). Tuck a granola bar or nuts in your bag to keep you going.

AND, MOST IMPORTANT,
after all your hard work, treat yourself to a refreshing cocktail!

gin drinks

Coco's Pearls
SERVES 4

A girl should be two things—classy and fabulous, like Coco Chanel and her pearls. This is an easy cocktail to whip up—just the thing while trying to be more of both.

8 oz. (237ml) gin
4 oz. (118ml) triple sec
2 oz. (59ml) freshly squeezed lemon juice
1 cup ice

● Pour ingredients into a cocktail shaker filled with ice. Mix well. Strain into martini glasses and serve.

shoes
Spectacular pumps with ankle straps.

Gin Press

SERVES 4

shoes
Ballet flats—let's
be safe while
commandeering a
hot iron.

Yes, it's true. I love to iron. There's nothing like a good press every now and then to make a girl happy. But you must have the right cocktail, or there won't be enough steam to get through the task. Sip, steam and repeat as necessary.

8 oz. (237ml) gin

4 oz. (118ml) Grand Marnier

2 oz. (59ml) freshly squeezed lime juice

1 cup ice

Lemon-flavored seltzer to top

4 lime slices for garnish

4 orange slices for garnish

● Mix gin, Grand Marnier and lime juice in a cocktail shaker filled with ice. Strain into martini glasses and top with seltzer. Garnish with fruit slices and serve.

gin drinks

Martini Classico
SERVES 4

The gin version—a girl has to have options.

8 oz. (237ml) gin
2 tablespoons (30ml) vermouth
1 cup ice
4 olives for garnish

● Mix gin and vermouth in an ice-filled shaker. Strain into martini glasses, garnish with olives and serve.

shoes
T-strap heels in chocolate brown or black.

The Dirty Girl is the same as the Martini Classico with a splash of olive juice added to the shaker. Sometimes it's necessary to get a little dirty.

Tina Collins

SERVES 4

Who needs Tom, anyway? This is what you drink when your jeans come out of the dryer looking like sticks instead of pants, requiring you to bust out your Tina Turner maneuvers to stretch them so that breathing—yours—can resume. If you're looking for a little pucker, substitute Collins mix for the sugar.

8 oz. (237ml) gin

2 oz. (59ml) freshly squeezed lemon juice

1 teaspoon (5ml) fine sugar

3 cups ice—1 for the shaker, 2 for the glasses

2 oz. (59ml) club soda

4 lemon wedges for garnish

● Pour gin, lemon juice and sugar into a cocktail shaker. Stir with a bar spoon and mix well until the sugar is dissolved. Add ice and shake vigorously. Strain mixture into ice-filled Collins glasses. Top with club soda, garnish with lemon wedges and serve.

shoes
Platform heels or boots with kick—make Tina proud.

Sunshine on Ice
Lady Rita

Happy Accident
South Beach
Slider

Tequila Kiss
Margarita

tequila

Thai One On
Diva's Dessert

On Parade
Holiday Helper
The Playdate

Jewel of India
Tequila Sunrise

tequila cocktails

Tequila is impetuous and dresses up in a flash. Off the cuff, on the fly, flirty, sexy—just like a bold piece of costume jewelry, sassy shoes or a colorful hobo bag—this is tequila.

Tequila is the perfect libation for impromptu parties, beach parties, dinner parties, dance parties, charity parties, birthday parties, holiday parties, you name it. Any kind of party is more festive with tequila. Call up a few friends, slip on that adorable number you picked up on the way home and mix up some Sunshine on Ice to get the party started in high style.

Bringing tequila to a party gets you invited back. Take along a pitcher full of sweet-and-salty Margaritas, and you're guaranteed to be on the guest list for the next do.

Jewel-toned tequila cocktails make festive additions to any breakfast or brunch get-together, and many times they turn breakfast into an all-day affair—in other words, they turn a Tequila Sunrise into a Tequila Sunset.

Because our lives, stylish as they may be, are moving faster and faster, take-out meals are becoming more and more frequent and popular. So I say if we're going to order in, we should do so in style. Whether it's Mexican, Chinese, Thai or a great all-American cheeseburger, a tequila cocktail makes even dinner from a bag fashionable. Try a Thai One On to complement pad thai and curry. Follow it up with a Diva's Dessert, and the meal is complete.

The tequila-drinking girl doesn't fuss over what she wears. She goes with her gut and pulls together a look quickly, always with fabulous results. You never overthink things while drinking tequila. The roast you were planning to wow with at the dinner party didn't turn out as planned? Serve your guests a few Happy Accidents, and they'll rave about your culinary prowess.

You can take risks with tequila—take that trip, wear those shoes, talk to that boy. Whatever you do, you'll pull it off—with style.

48

Sunshine on Ice
SERVES 4

A tasty, tangy accompaniment to coffee and croissants, they're packed with zesty grapefruit and lemon and are a delicious way to start your day.

8 oz. (237ml) tequila blanco

4 oz. (118ml) Grand Marnier

4 oz. (118ml) ruby-red grapefruit juice

2 oz. (59ml) freshly squeezed lemon juice

4 cups ice—2 for the pitcher, 2 for the glasses

Seltzer to top

4 grapefruit wedges for garnish

Shoes
Slingbacks in yellow or coral—add a clip-on gem or flower for extra morning charm.

● Pour tequila, Grand Marnier and grapefruit and lemon juices into a pitcher filled with ice. Stir the mixture well, pour into rocks glasses and top with seltzer. Garnish with grapefruit wedges and serve.

Lady Rita
SERVES 4

I recently made a big batch of violet-hued Lady Ritas for an impromptu Friday night "Ready for the Weekend" party with friends and neighbors. Pick up some fresh lavender from the grocery store, use some in the cocktail and put the rest in a small vase with ruby-red roses to get the weekend started in fine fashion!

8 oz. (237ml) tequila blanco

4 oz. (118ml) Marie Brizard parfait amour

2 oz. (59ml) freshly squeezed lemon juice

2 oz. (59ml) simple syrup*

1 cup ice

4 fresh lavender buds for garnish

● Pour all liquid ingredients into a pitcher half-filled with ice. Mix well. Strain into martini glasses. Garnish with lavender buds and serve.

*recipe on page 134

shoes

Pumps—suede for fall/winter, linen for spring/summer—give me a lift and help me forget my weekday pressures.

Happy Accident

SERVES 4

I threw together this delicious concoction to distract guests from an overcooked rack of lamb. Once everyone tasted the tequila and smelled the rosemary, they thought the lamb was the culinary highlight of the year. I make Happy Accidents all the time now. And to think they were born out of a dire situation!

2 rosemary sprigs

8 oz. (237ml) tequila blanco

4 oz. (118ml) limoncello

2 oz. (59ml) freshly squeezed lemon juice

2 oz. (59ml) freshly squeezed lime juice

2 cups ice

8 oz. (237ml) lime-flavored seltzer

● Place the rosemary sprigs in a pitcher. Pour in tequila, limoncello and juices. Muddle the rosemary to release its flavor. Let the mixture sit for a few minutes to let the flavors marry. Strain into ice-filled rocks glasses. Top with seltzer and serve.

shoes
Open-toe heels in a bright color, like red or peacock blue, let people notice your shoes, not your rack.

tequila cocktails

South Beach Slider
SERVES 4

Jello shots are back in fashion, big-time!
They're the perfect party fare. Let
someone else bring the cheese
and crackers.

8 oz. (237ml) boiling water

1 box cranberry gelatin

4 oz. (118ml) tequila or vodka

2 oz. (59ml) Grand Marnier

2 oz. (59ml) freshly squeezed lime juice

● In a small bowl, mix boiling water and
gelatin. Stir until gelatin dissolves. Let
stand until it comes to room temperature.
Pour into a cocktail shaker, add remaining
ingredients and shake well. Pour evenly
into mini glasses and serve.

shoes
Flip-flops
embellished with
gems are ideal for
sliding around
the party in
style.

52

Citrus-toned espadrilles are made for rest and relaxation.

Tequila Kiss

SERVES 4

Bursting with citrus tones and vitamin C, this concoction is like a mini spa treatment!

8 oz. (237ml) tequila blanco

2 oz. (59ml) freshly squeezed lime juice

2 oz. (59ml) freshly squeezed lemon juice

2 oz. (59ml) ruby-red grapefruit juice

1 cup ice

● Mix all ingredients in a cocktail shaker filled with ice. Pour evenly into mini glasses and serve.

Tequila is the classic shot. The South Beach Slider and the Tequila Kiss drt up and turn it into something much more stylish.

which stylish girl are you?

There is no one way to be stylish. Each of us has our own unique style that is an extension of our personalities, but there are a few categories that most of us fit into somewhere. Check out the list below to see which cocktail best fits your style. And, of course, if your look spans more than one category, feel free to try more than one cocktail!

The Lady
Unabashedly feminine, your style is demure but fun and never stodgy. If you could visit any period in fashion history, it would be the 1950s, with its full skirts, heels and ladylike gloves.
YOUR COCKTAIL: The Slicker *page 19*

The Maverick
Not afraid to experiment and never a slave to the latest trends, you make your own style. It's no surprise when people copy *your* look.
YOUR COCKTAIL: Mai Tai *page 78*

The Minimalist
Featuring simple shapes, neutrals, and monochromatic palettes, your clothing style extends to your home décor. Your wardrobe is pared down to just the absolute essentials, pieces that work perfectly for you and nothing extraneous.
YOUR COCKTAIL: Just Peachy *page 97*

The Eclectic

You love mixing styles, even eras, combining new and vintage pieces to create your own statement. What you choose to wear varies from day to day—it all depends on your mood!

YOUR COCKTAIL: Springtime in Paris *page 101*

The Bohemian

Mixing elements of hippie, gypsy and ethnic styles, boho-chic is updated and modern. Your look is casual and effortless, but not sloppy, in vibrant colors and prints embellished with dangling earrings and stacks of bangles.

YOUR COCKTAIL: Margarita *page 56*

The Bombshell

You're not afraid to turn heads. Sexy, but never over the top, you show off your curves in form-fitting, feminine styles. High heels, red lipstick and just a touch of cleavage complete the look.

YOUR COCKTAIL: Mango Mojito *page 75*

Classic Chic

Polished and pulled-together, you exude class and elegance. You're effortlessly chic in simple, but high-quality pieces. Timeless, yet anything but boring, your look never goes out of style.

YOUR COCKTAIL: Limetini *page 38*

tequila cocktails

Margarita
SERVES 4

This is the classic tequila cocktail.
Make a pitcherful and have friends over
for tasty guac from a box.

4 cups crushed ice
8 oz. (237ml) tequila blanco
2 oz. (59ml) Grand Marnier
4 oz. (118ml) key lime juice
4 lime wedges for garnish,
1 for the glass rims
Kosher salt (optional)

shoes:
Warm months—
open-toe mules;
cooler months—soft
leather riding boots
in cognac.

● In a pitcher or cocktail shaker filled
with ice, mix tequila, Grand Marnier and
lime juice. Stir vigorously, allowing the
flavors to marry and chill. Pour into
glasses. Add more crushed ice if
necessary. Garnish with lime wedges.

FOR SALTED RIMS:
Rub the rims of the glasses
with lime wedge. Dip the rims into
a small plate of kosher salt.

Thai One On
SERVES 4

This refreshing blend of tequila and fruit juices nicely complements the lemongrass/coconut/curry flavors of Southeast Asian food.

8 oz. (237ml) tequila blanco
4 oz. (118ml) pink grapefruit juice
2 oz. (59ml) freshly squeezed lime juice
4 oz. (118ml) apricot nectar
3 cups ice
4 lime wedges for garnish

● Mix tequila, juices and nectar in a large pitcher filled with ice. Allow 3 minutes for flavors to marry and chill. Strain into white wine glasses, garnish with lime wedges and serve.

Shoes
Black suede boots.

Diva's Dessert
SERVES 4

A favorite for burger and DVD night. After ordering cheeseburgers from your joint of choice, put in a movie and snuggle up with one of these. Smooth and decadent, it's dessert in a glass.

4 oz. (118ml) tequila blanco
2 oz. (59ml) Kahlúa
2 oz. (59ml) Baileys Irish Cream
2 oz. (59ml) prepared espresso
1 cup ice

shoes
Fancy slippers with cinematic style.

● Pour all ingredients into a cocktail shaker filled with ice. Shake vigorously. Strain into martini glasses and serve.

Wine and beer aren't the only beverages that pair well with food. Tequila cocktails, from the classic Margarita to the Thai One On to the Diva's Dessert, are delicious alternatives.

Jewel of India
SERVES 4

My friend Karina hosts a benefit every year to help build schools in India. She holds it in her garden with tables layered in jewel-toned sarongs and flowers in bright hues and crystal chandeliers hung from tree branches. I bring the cocktail fixings, and it turns into a fabulous afternoon of sharing, caring and celebrating. And that is so very stylish.

shoes
Strappy, jewel-toned sandals.

8 oz. (237ml) tequila blanco

8 oz. (237ml) mango nectar

4 oz. (118ml) freshly squeezed orange juice

2 cups ice

4 oz. (118ml) Prosecco, chilled

4 orange slices for garnish

● Mix tequila, mango nectar and orange juice in a pitcher filled with ice. Pour mixture into white wine glasses and top with Prosecco. Garnish with orange slices and serve.

Tequila Sunrise
SERVES 4

I served these at a going-away party for dear friends who were moving back to London, so that whenever they drank them in the future, they would always think of the old gang and know that we're just a sunrise away. You can make the base cocktail ahead of time and then add the "sunrise" right before you serve!

shoes
Ballet flats in a citrus color—even better in polka dots, stripes or plaid.

4 cups ice—1 for the pitcher, 3 for the glasses

8 oz. (237ml) tequila blanco

16 oz. (½ liter) freshly squeezed orange juice

2 oz. (59ml) freshly squeezed lime juice

4 orange wedges for garnish

2 oz. (59ml) grenadine

● Into a pitcher half-filled with ice, pour tequila and orange and lime juices. Stir well. Pour the mixture evenly into ice-filled highball glasses. Garnish with orange wedges. Just before serving, slowly add the grenadine, dividing evenly between glasses. It will sink, then float to the top, creating a sunrise effect.

On Parade

SERVES 4

Don't you just love a parade? And small
towns that have them for every occasion?
I have served this drink after a Memorial Day
parade and added blue star-shaped ice cubes
(made with blue Curaçao), and after a
Halloween parade with ice cubes infested with
spiders (plastic ones, of course!).

8 oz. (237ml) tequila blanco
4 oz. (118ml) limoncello
2 oz. (59ml) freshly squeezed lemon juice
4 oz. (118ml) grenadine
1 teaspoon (5ml) fine sugar
1 cup ice
Club soda to top

● Pour all of the ingredients
except the club soda into a pitcher
half-filled with ice. Mix well. Pour
evenly into white wine glasses, top
with club soda and serve.

61

Shoes
Patriotic espadrilles
for Memorial Day;
knee-high boots
for Halloween.

Holiday Helper
SERVES 4

Tequila is what you serve your girlfriends when they come over for online holiday shopping. I started this tradition last year, because six savvy shoppers are better than one. These delectable drinks help you focus on the task of finding the spot-on gift for everyone while having fun. Now that's successful shopping.

8 oz. (237ml) tequila blanco

4 oz. (118ml) ruby-red grapefruit juice

4 oz. (118ml) raspberry liqueur

2 oz. (59ml) freshly squeezed lemon juice

5 cups ice—3 for the pitcher,
2 for the glasses

4 lemon slices for garnish

shoes
Sequined slippers are comfy and festive.

● Mix all ingredients in a large pitcher filled with ice. Pour into ice-filled rocks glasses. Garnish with lemon slices and serve.

You'll be the most stylish mom in the room in your suede ankle boots.

The Playdate

SERVES 4

Just the thing on a wintery afternoon when you have friends and their kids over. Make a pitcher of these for the adults and a pitcher of apricot nectar and seltzer for the kiddies!

63

8 oz. (237ml) tequila blanco

4 oz. (118ml) pear brandy

8 oz. (237ml) apricot nectar

4 oz. (118ml) lime juice

3 cups ice

● Mix all ingredients in a large pitcher filled with ice. Pour into rocks glasses and serve.

Frozen Rum Runner
A Little
Dinghy

Captain's
Delight
Cabana 24

Rum Swizzle
Rum Punch
Strawberry
Mojito

rum

Blueberry
Mojito
Frozen Mango
Mojito

Caipirinha
Island Time

Mai Tai
Berry Daquiri

rum drinks

Rum is like the perfect basic outfit that just needs a few accessories—
wide belt, chunky necklace, irresistible boots—to complete it. It needs
a little kicker, like fruit, juice, fruit liqueur or, at times, more rum!

Native to the warm climes of the Caribbean and South America, rum is made for relaxation, like a long flowing sundress or short shorts. Rum is what you drink when you don't have to be alert for the rest of the afternoon, when you can just sip your piña colada or daiquiri and take in the spirits and sugar with abandon.

When long, sunny days melt into soft summer nights, when all you have to do is what you want to and there's no place you have to be, a rum cocktail is the perfect accompaniment. When your appetite fades under the day's hot sun and thirst increases, you want something cool, maybe frozen, with a citrusy tang, a sweet finish and a straw for easy sipping. You can't go wrong with a piña colada (the Cabana 24 is my take on this classic).

Rum is what you drink when you're poolside, dockside, beachside, or in general beside yourself. While indulging in rum, cover up in a tropical-toned tunic for glamour and comfort!

Rum is perfect for easy summer entertaining, beach parties, beach days, trips to the beach or beach houses. A big batch of Rum Punch will let you play hostess with breezy style.

Rum is what to drink when you're on a boat—a big one, little one, sailboat, yacht, fishing boat, speedboat—as a passenger, of course. Running a boat is a lot of work (what with all those lines and jibbing and coming about), so it helps to have a captain, especially if you want to enjoy a delicious Rum Runner while onboard.

Rum is trendy and sexy and is working its way into our chic cocktail bars. When day turns to night and you're ready to heat things up, keep your cool with a mint-infused Mojito.

Like rum, style has no borders. Wherever you go, be sure to bring it with you.

Frozen Rum Runner
SERVES 4

The Rum Runner is famous down Key Largo
way. Try mixing up a batch on a hot, sticky
afternoon. My brothers always serve Rum
Runners with seafood, fresh shrimp or clams
on the half-shell to remind themselves of
floating on a boat in the Keys.

6 oz. (177ml) dark rum

4 oz. (118ml) blackberry brandy

2 oz. (59ml) banana liqueur

2 oz. (59ml) freshly squeezed lime juice

Splash of grenadine

3 cups ice

8 fresh blackberries for garnish

4 lime slices for garnish

4 straws

● Mix all liquid ingredients in a blender filled
with ice. Blend until smooth. Pour evenly into
highball glasses. Garnish with fresh blackberries
and lime slices. Add straws and serve.

67

rum drinks

shoes

Slip-on mules
in a fun,
fashion-forward
pattern.

A Little Dinghy
SERVES 4

Always wear fabulous shoes, even on
a boat. Just in case they require removal
before boarding, make sure you've
had a pedicure.

4 oz. (118ml) Bacardi Limón rum

4 oz. (118ml) Chambord liqueur

2 oz. (59ml) freshly squeezed lemon juice

3 cups ice—1 for shaker, 2 for glasses

8 oz. (237ml) Prosecco to top

● Pour the rum, Chambord and
lemon juice into a cocktail shaker
filled with ice and mix well.
Distribute the mixture evenly into
ice-filled lowball glasses, top
with Prosecco and serve.

Rum
is what you
drink when you're
feeling the music—
island music, calypso
tunes, music with a
tropical beat, anything
with a little rhythm,
really.

68

Shoes
Sexy seaside-
inspired sandals
with a stacked
wedge heel.

Captain's Delight
SERVES 4

I used to serve these on my rooftop when
I lived in Manhattan. If you turned in a
particular direction you could see the
Hudson River. Cocktails on my roof became
a Thursday after-work tradition with friends
and colleagues.

8 oz. (237ml) Captain Morgan
Parrot Bay Coconut rum

4 oz. (118ml) white rum

8 oz. (237ml) pineapple juice

4 oz. (118ml) cranberry juice

2 oz. (59ml) freshly squeezed lime juice

2 cups ice

4 lime slices for garnish

● Pour all ingredients into a pitcher filled
with ice. Mix well and pour into highball
glasses. Garnish with lime slices and serve.

69

Cabana 24
SERVES 4

This colorful concoction reminds me of rows of cabanas painted in bright colors at a beach club where piña coladas are served all day.

2 oz. (59ml) white rum

4 oz. (118ml) pineapple juice

2 oz. (59ml) Coco Lopez cream of coconut

2 oz. (59ml) passion fruit nectar

2 oz. (59ml) key lime juice

3 cups ice

4 pineapple chunks for garnish

4 lime slices for garnish

4 straws

shoes

Tropical-toned Jack Rogers sandals that match the cabana.

● Combine all ingredients except garnishes in a blender filled with ice and mix until smooth, about 1 minute. Pour evenly into Hurricane glasses. Garnish with pineapple chunks and lime slices. Add a festive straw to each and serve.

Brightly colored
Capri sandals
sizzle.

Rum Swizzle
SERVES 4

The swizzle hails from Bermuda. I put a tropical spin on it, substituting passion-fruit nectar for the traditional bitters and sugar. I say if you're going to swizzle, make it sizzle!

8 oz. (237ml) soda water

2 oz. (59ml) freshly squeezed lime juice

4 oz. (118ml) passion-fruit nectar

2 cups ice

8 oz. (237ml) dark rum

8 lime wedges for garnish

4 sugared swizzle sticks

● In a pitcher, mix soda water, lime juice and passion-fruit nectar. Divide equally among ice-filled lowball glasses. Top with rum and garnish with lime wedges. Add swizzle sticks and serve.

rum drinks

Rum Punch
SERVES 4

Intensely flavorful and perfect by the pitcherful, a flavor-packed punch is the ultimate party drink. It's easy for guests to serve themselves, so you get to relax and enjoy. I just love a self-serve bar.

8 oz. (237ml) pineapple juice

4 oz. (118ml) orange juice

8 oz. (237ml) white rum

4 oz. (118ml) blackberry brandy

2 oz. (59ml) grenadine

2 oz. (59ml) freshly squeezed lime juice

2 oz. (59ml) Coco Lopez cream of coconut

3 cups ice

4 pineapple chunks for garnish

4 cherries for garnish

4 straws

shoes
High-heeled espadrilles pack a punch.

● Mix all ingredients in a large pitcher filled with ice. Pour into hurricane glasses. Garnish with pineapple and cherries. Add a straw to each glass and serve.

Strawberry Mojito
SERVES 4

Mojitos are my current cocktail obsession.
If you don't already have one, get yourself a
muddler—a must-have tool for the bar—and
start mixing up these Cuban delights.

10 mint leaves, plus 4 more for garnish
10 lime slices (about 2 limes)
10 strawberries, diced
2 oz. (59ml) simple syrup*
8 oz. (237ml) white rum
2 oz. (59ml) freshly squeezed lime juice
2 cups ice
4 oz. (118ml) seltzer to top

● In a cocktail shaker or bar glass, combine mint
leaves, lime slices and strawberries. Muddle
ingredients well with a muddler or bar spoon to
release flavors. Add simple syrup, rum and lime
juice and shake well. Pour mixture into lowball
glasses. Add ice and top with seltzer. Garnish
with fresh mint leaves and serve.

*recipe on page 134

73

rum drinks

Blueberry Mojito
SERVES 4

Bursting with fresh blueberries and mint, these lovely libations are a pleasure to behold and to drink.

10 mint leaves

10 lime slices (about 2 limes)—6 for the cocktails, 4 for garnish

1 cup fresh blueberries

2 oz. (59ml) simple syrup*

4 oz. (118ml) fresh lime juice

8 oz. (237ml) white rum

2 cups ice cubes

4 oz. (118ml) seltzer to top

shoes
Sexy slides in a hot color.

● In a cocktail shaker or bar glass, combine mint leaves, lime slices and blueberries. Muddle ingredients well with a muddler or bar spoon to release the flavors. Add simple syrup, lime juice and rum. Shake well. Pour mixture into lowball glasses. Add ice and top with seltzer. Garnish with lime slices and serve.

*see recipe on page 134

Frozen Mango Mojito
SERVES 4

shoes
Patent-leather thong sandals— they'll shine just like you!

Tantalizingly cool with a citrus bite, this cocktail fits the bill for a day at the beach or a late-afternoon cool-down.

10 mint leaves

2 cups fresh or frozen mango

2 oz. (59ml) simple syrup*

2 oz. (59ml) freshly squeezed lime juice

8 oz. (237ml) white rum

3 cups ice cubes

4 lime wedges for garnish

4 straws

75

● In a blender, place mint leaves, mango, simple syrup, lime juice, rum and ice cubes. Blend until smooth. Pour mixture into highball glasses. Garnish with lime wedges, add straws and serve.

*see recipe on page 134

Fresh pre-cut and packaged mango is often available in the produce section of local markets. Save yourself some work so you have more time to enjoy your creation!

rum drinks

Caipirinha
SERVES 4

Caipirinha...the name alone sounds like an exotic dance. And dance you will after having a few of these. A luscious combination of rum, lime and sugar, this is the national cocktail of Brazil.

3 limes, cut into wedges—12 for the cocktails, 4 for garnish
6 teaspoons (30g) fine sugar
8 oz. (237ml) cachaça
2 cups ice
4 oz. (118ml) seltzer to top (optional)

● Place the lime wedges and sugar in a small pitcher. Use a muddler or bar spoon to mash the lime and sugar together. Add the rum and stir. Add the ice and stir again, allowing the flavors to blend together for a few minutes. Pour into lowball glasses, garnish with lime wedges and serve. Top with seltzer if desired.

shoes
Brightly colored Havaiana flip-flops.

Traditionally made with cachaça, the Caipirinha is just as delicious with rum, which is easier to find stateside.

Island Time

SERVES 4

Heavenly on lazy, hot and hazy
weekend days. Mix up a batch of these
for an instant pool party.

8 oz. (237ml) Captain Morgan
Parrot Bay Coconut rum

4 oz. (118ml) freshly squeezed
orange juice

4 oz. (118ml) fresh strawberry juice

3 cups crushed ice

8 mint leaves for garnish

● Pour all the liquid ingredients into
a pitcher half-filled with crushed ice. Mix
well. Pour evenly into highball glasses,
garnish with mint leaves and serve.

Shoes

Open-toes, because
with all the muddling
you'll be doing,
you'll need to keep
your toes cool.

rum drinks

Mai Tai
SERVES 4

Razzle-dazzle 'em with this tropical
concoction. Color is key, so load up on
the umbrellas and straws and mix up
a batch of these party-starters.

4 oz. (118ml) white rum

4 oz. (118ml) dark rum

4 oz. (118ml) pineapple juice

2 oz. (59ml) clear Curaçao

2 oz. (59ml) freshly squeezed lime juice

2 oz. (59ml) grenadine

4 cups ice—2 for the pitcher, 2 for the glasses

4 cherries for garnish

4 lime slices for garnish

4 straws

4 mini umbrellas

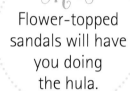

shoes
Flower-topped
sandals will have
you doing
the hula.

● Pour all liquid ingredients into a pitcher,
add ice and mix thoroughly. Let the
flavors marry for about 3 minutes. Pour
into ice-filled highball glasses. Garnish with
cherries and lime slices. Add straws and/or
umbrellas and serve.

Berry Daquiri

SERVES 4

It may be the classic, but you don't
have to limit yourself to strawberries.
Use whichever berries are in season, or
combine a few for a berrylicious drink.

8 oz. (237ml) white rum

1 cup (237ml) mixed fresh berries
(strawberries, raspberries, blueberries and/or
blackberries), plus 12–16 for garnish

2 oz. (59ml) freshly squeezed lime juice

2 oz. (59ml) simple syrup*

3 cups ice

4 straws

● Place all the ingredients in a blender
and fill with ice. Blend until smooth,
about 1 minute. Pour into tall hurricane
glasses, garnish with a few berries, add
a straw and serve.

*see recipe on page 134

79

drinkstrology

What does my future hold? Will I find true love? What cocktail should I try? It's all written in the stars. Take a cue from a savvy astrologist to find your cocktail match made in heaven.

Aries (March 21–April 19)

● Looking for a cocktail to suit your impulsive Aries nature? Search no further than the vibrant red-to-gold hue of the **Tequila Sunrise** (page 60). Rams are full of the joys of spring as winter fades, a new day dawns and a new cycle kicks in. Your enthusiasm bubbles over as the action begins, but watch out—boredom sometimes rears its ugly head before you get to the final lap. With the lovely glow of this cocktail, you can't help but focus on the golden goal at the top of the glass. Go for the full package and drape yourself in a matching tie-dyed swirl of silk.

FAVORITE BOOK: *Tequila Mockingbird*, of course

Taurus (April 20–May 20)

● As earthy, tactile Taurus, you love the sensual delights of a ripe vegetable tantalizing your taste buds—in liquid form, of course. What better cocktail to tempt the tongue than the rich bullfighter-red **Bloody Mary** (page 27)? The salt of the earth, the floppy-topped celery leaf, the sun-kissed lemon and that teeniest hint of fiery Tabasco all combine with vodka and tomato to put a seductive skip in your step. But don't even think of ordering this divine taste sensation unless you're sporting a floor-length blood-red cape in the finest of fabrics.

FAVORITE SONG: "Will You Still Love Me, Tomato?"

Gemini (May 21–June 20)

● Fabulous? Gemini? Always! You're all out there, every day, every minute! Places to go, people to meet...making the most of every situation as you flit from one social scene to the next. What cocktail better reflects your butterfly nature than the zingy **Manhattan** (page 118)? Named after the center of "the city that never sleeps," the smooth jazz note of whisky swirled with the zesty peel of puckering oranges keeps your Gemini lines of communication open and ready for business. A jaunty beret perched atop your well-coiffed head echoes the perky cherry atop your stylish cocktail.

CATCH PHRASE: "I'll have what she's having!"

Cancer (June 21–July 22)

● Nothing says "I'm home" like the humble **Limetini** (page 38), and no one loves home more than you, enchanting Cancerian. Imagine, if you will: After a hard day at the office, you walk in the door, sashay over to the cocktail cabinet and tinkle some ice cubes in a tumbler. Add a good slosh of gin and a generous dash of lime juice and top it off with a splash of simple syrup. Marvelous! Then throw on a filmy peignoir and drape yourself over the couch. Put feet up, take giant sip, pick up phone, order pizza. Nothing could be simpler. ultraviolet lights to get the full lunar effect.

FAVORITE SONG: "Moon Quiver"

Leo (July 23–August 22)

● The sun, like Leo, is the center of attention when it comes to this planet, so here we need a cocktail that demands respect, that glows with the fire and passion that is your true Leo nature. What better golden delight than the salty-maned **Margarita** (page 56), with its solar tequila base mixed with zesty, juicy lime? "Drink me, I'm fabulous" is the gutsy cry of both your not-to-be-ignored sign and this tastefest of a cocktail. Ensure that your diamante-encrusted outfit gets maximum sparkle by positioning yourself in the best light.

FAVORITE MUSICIAN: Jimmy Buffett (you know why)

Virgo (August 23–September 22)

● Sophisticated, no-nonsense, attractive, straight-up, perfect—a description of both you, lovely Virgo, and the even lovelier **Martini Classico** (pages 13 and 44). A little complicated at first...what to choose? Gin? Vodka? Shaken? Stirred? Olive? No olive? Sunny-side up? Over easy? Eeeek! But...once you break the code, you won't look back. Being slightly fastidious, you'll love the martini even more once you get it right. Nothing less than a velvet tuxedo with a feminine twist will do while quaffing this luxurious beverage. If it's good enough for James Bond....

FAVORITE SWIMSUIT: Martini weeny yellow polka dot bikini

Libra (September 23–October 22)

● "What will I drink tonight?" Red or white? Maybe rosé! You are versatile, Libra, but some say you can be a bit of a fence-sitter—a tasteful one, of course. With your grace and discernment, you're perfectly in tune with the beverage that is wine. There's no reason for indecision—hot and sunny poolside dining cries out for a chilled sauvignon blanc, freshly carved roast beef begs a hearty cab sav—but if you really can't make up your mind, there's always **The Ginger** (page 93) to add some sparkle to your day. Perfect red nails peeping from a white satin gauntlet and wrapped around a crystal stem—sooo very Libra.

FAVORITE BOOK: *Red Is From Mars, White Is From Venus*

Scorpio (October 23–November 21)

● You have a powerful magnetism, Scorpio, so you deserve a cocktail that

screams exotic passion and explosive allure. The **Kir Royale** (page 104) has all the fizz and bubble of world-class champagne with the color and flavor of crème de cassis thrown in to suggest the mystery and desire that is so Scorpio. Mmmm—love those bubbles! Add a fresh blackberry to pump it up—and a BlackBerry to call your friends for a party. Throw on a pair of killer black heels to amp up your sex appeal as you welcome guests to your lair.
FAVORITE MOVIE: *Shampoo*

Sagittarius (November 22–December 21)

● You're friendly and philosophical, Sagittarius, and your cosmopolitan lifestyle is full of travel, study and interesting people. The sophisticated **Cosmopolitan** (page 29) works well with your larger-than-life freedom-loving character. "Give me vodka," you say, "give me Cointreau, cranberry, lime, history, politics, news, views, everything—I want it all! And while you're at it, give me a horse. After all, I am the centaur!" As you don't have the legs of a centaur, you'll need a sporty pair of moleskin jodhpurs to underline your equine connections.
FAVORITE CROP: Riding

Capricorn (December 22–January 19)

● Sitting firm on the bar stool, you make calls, seal deals, take sips. You mean business, Capricorn, and you're not one to embellish, so when you're out for a night on the town, it means shots are the go-to libation—just pure, unadulterated fun in a glass. The **Prêt-à-Party** (page 22), the **Lemon Drop** (page 24)—name your shot,

you can handle it. Now, who would guess that under your finely cut Chanel suit lies an homage to Victoria's Secret in black lace and ribbon?
FAVORITE SHOT: From the hip

Aquarius (January 20–February 18)

● As the free-spirited water bearer, you need the flavors of the beach to really feel at home. The **Cabana 24** (page 70) is all that and more as it wraps your Aquarian taste buds in folds of pirate rum, zingy pineapple and cream of coconut. Feel the wind in your hair and the waves lapping your toes as you pensively stride along the seafront in your diaphanous white cotton shift, drink in one hand, grains of sand in the other. That teeny paper parasol is never going to keep the sun off your face, so make sure you're wearing some red-hot Ray-Bans for added protection.
FAVORITE HAT: Carmen Miranda's banana boat hat, of course.

Pisces (February 19–March 20)

● The vibrant, poetic heart of Pisces will best be served by dabbling in a delicious **Berry Daiquiri** (page 79), especially if a strawberry or two is dropped casually in the glass. The sassy kick of rum belies the sweetness of tongue-tingling lime and sugar that swirl recklessly around the Piscean mouth. Those lips were made for puckering, so make sure your lipstick is perfectly matched to those strawberries for ultimate fashionista appeal!
FAVORITE SONG: "Daquiris Are a Girl's Best Friend"

Tropical
Sangria
Sangria Bonita

Harvest-Punch
Slopeside

wine

Girly-Girl
Sherry Girl

The Ginger
Sock It to Me
Just Peachy

wine cocktails

I can't say enough good things about wine: It comes in several colors, it's derived from grapes and it's good for your health, helping to lower your cholesterol and blood pressure and probably taking care of anything else that ails you. It's kind of like Botox in a glass. Most important, it's delicious.

Wine is probably the most versatile cocktail base. Like a pair of great jeans, it goes with everything. Dress it up or dress it down: For a glamorous occasion, try the Ginger. When you want to kick back, you can't go wrong with sangria.

You can get by quite well with two pairs of denim: skinny jeans to tuck into boots or wear with flats and long, straight-legged jeans to don with heels. Likewise, there are two main types of wine—red and white—that will keep you busy mixing cocktails for a long time. But there are so many fun variations on basic red and white that it would be a shame to stop there. Rosé, Prosecco, sake, sherry...the list goes on. While you're at it, pick up a couple more styles of jeans to make sure you're covered.

Wine is the perfect everyday libation. Drink it when you meet the girls for lunch, friends after work or your husband for dinner. Wine is great in the tub, in the Jacuzzi, at poolside. It's the ideal drink when you're curled up watching a movie, reading a good book or (most essential) trying to write a book.

Wine is made for clubbing—for the book club, craft club, personal finance club, movie club, and my favorite, the hire-a-sitter-and-meet-your-friends-out-for-a-glass-of-wine club.

Wine is the perfect accompaniment to every food group, from cheese to salads to pastas to beef to fish to dessert, from start to finish. With wine, you're ready for any and every situation.

wine is easy—it goes down smooth, gives you a burst of energy, then mellows out for a fine finish, and it keeps you wanting more.

Harvest-Punch

SERVES 4

My cousin Kim is the events director at a vineyard where she recently threw a fabulous fête. She had an assortment of cheeses and breads on rustic tables with sunflowers, chocolate dahlias, orange roses and deep blue hydrangeas, all arranged in old wine boxes. As we chatted and mingled in our fall fashion best, we sipped this sublime cocktail, which Kim served in a big green glass drinks dispenser. It sure beat the water cooler!

8 oz. (237ml) Port wine

4 oz. (118ml) Grand Marnier

4 oz. (118ml) Amaretto di Saronno

2 cups ice

2 small oranges, thinly sliced

shoes

Olive suede ankle boots are perfect for tripping among the vines.

● Pour all liquid ingredients into a pitcher filled with ice and mix well. Secure one orange slice on the rim of each of 4 red wine goblets for garnish. Add the remaining slices to the pitcher. Pour into glasses and serve.

wine cocktails

Slopeside
SERVES 4

After hitting the slopes, nothing warms you
like a pitcher of these dandies. The hints of
blackberry set off the deep flavors of the
cabernet wine to perfection. Bring them out
to the hot tub for unparalleled slope style!

1 bottle (750ml) cabernet
8 oz. (237ml) crème de cassis
8 oz. (237ml) lemon-flavored
seltzer
4 berry-flavored swizzle sticks

shoes
Furry boots will keep
your feet toasty,
while the cocktail
takes care of
the rest!

● In a glass pitcher, pour wine and
crème de cassis. Top off with seltzer, then
pour into red wine goblets. Garnish with
berry-flavored swizzle sticks and serve.

For parties,
save yourself time
and effort by using
a large drinks dispenser. And
if you buy your supplies in
bulk, you can use the
savings to expand your
shoe collection!

88

Tropical Sangria
SERVES 4

A batch of this summery libation is ideal on warm nights on the beach. The brandy-soaked fruit takes this celebrated wine concoction to a whole new level.

1 ripe mango
1 lime
1 lemon
½ pineapple
3 kiwis
1 starfruit
8 oz. (237ml) Grand Marnier
1 bottle (750ml) dry white wine
3 cups ice

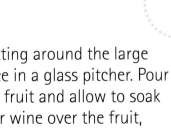

Shoes
Sandals with sass.

● Slice the fruit, cutting around the large mango pit, and place in a glass pitcher. Pour Grand Marnier over fruit and allow to soak for 10 minutes. Pour wine over the fruit, add ice and serve in white wine glasses.

Sangria Bonita
SERVES 4

This is a fabulous warm-weather drink. Mixed in a pitcher filled with ice, it practically serves itself!

Shoes
Open-toe wedges will take you from patio to deck.

4 oz. (118ml) vodka

4 oz. (118ml) Tuaca liqueur

8 oz. (237ml) Cointreau

8 oz. (237ml) white cranberry juice

1 bottle (750ml) Prosecco

4 sprigs mint

12 fresh strawberries with tops cut off

8 starfruit slices

● Combine vodka, Tuaca, Cointreau and juice in a large glass pitcher. Chill for a few hours, allowing the flavors to marry. Add Prosecco and pour into red wine goblets. Garnish with mint sprigs, fresh strawberries and starfruit and serve.

Girly-Girl
SERVES 4

This cocktail is pink perfection and has become a staple for girly parties like bridal showers. But don't let the lack of an occasion stop you from celebrating!

8 oz. (237ml) sauvignon blanc
4 oz. (118ml) Hennessy XO cognac
1 cup ice
Champagne to top
4 sugar cubes
Small amount bitters

● In a cocktail shaker, pour wine and cognac. Add ice and let chill. Place one sugar cube each in bottom of 4 champagne flutes and add a few drops of bitters to each. Strain mixture into flutes, then top with champagne. Serve.

Sherry Girl

SERVES 4

I serve this festive cocktail at the birthday club my girlfriends and I have every time one of us celebrates a birthday. We rotate houses, and we all bring a dish, from starters to mains to dessert, and of course, a cocktail to start! We get dressed up in something fancy and meet up for a fine evening.

8 oz. (237ml) dry sherry

2 oz. (59ml) apricot nectar

2 oz. (59ml) triple sec

2 oz. (59ml) freshly squeezed lemon juice

1 cup ice

● Pour all the ingredients into a cocktail shaker filled with ice and mix well. Pour cocktails into rocks glasses and serve.

shoes
Violet-hued
Mary Janes.

Shoes
Solid-colored pumps
with a clip. Clips are
back in fashion, and I
have a closet full of
happy shoes!

The Ginger
SERVES 4

Aptly named for the oh-so-glam
island girl. If only we all could look that
good while stranded on an island.

2 cups ice
4 oz. (118ml) Absolut Citron vodka
4 oz. (118ml) Grand Marnier
4 oz. (118ml) peach or apricot nectar
1 bottle (750ml) Prosecco, chilled

● In a glass pitcher filled with ice, mix
the vodka, Grand Marnier and nectar.
Let the mixture chill and allow the flavors
to marry for 3 minutes. Strain ice. Add
chilled Prosecco. Pour into white wine
glasses and serve.

movie night match-up

One of my favorite excuses to have the girls over for cocktails is Movie Night! It's a great time to catch up with friends and check out a new flick or revisit an old favorite. I pick a film, choose a cocktail to fit the theme and whip up a variety of snacks to round out the evening. Here are a few foolproof choices.
Kleenex optional.

GONE WITH THE WIND 1939
Scarlet O'Hara was cinema's original stylish girl. She didn't let a little thing like the Civil War cramp her style. (Curtains are wasted on windows anyway.)
COCKTAIL: Kir Royale (page 104).

CASABLANCA 1942
Set in World War II Morocco, this tale of ill-fated lovers is one of the most excruciatingly romantic films of all time. Ingrid Bergman never looked better than in her flawless suits and hats.
COCKTAIL: Dirty Girl (page 44).

BREAKFAST AT TIFFANY'S 1961
Holly Golightly was Audrey Hepburn's signature role and established the style with which she is so closely identified. Women have been trying to copy it ever since.
COCKTAIL: Manhattan (page 118).

ROMAN HOLIDAY 1953
This classic introduced American audiences to movie and style icon Audrey Hepburn, who plays a princess trying to experience life incognito in Rome.
COCKTAIL: The Confession (page 39).

BAREFOOT IN THE PARK 1967
Who can resist Jane Fonda and Robert Redford as the quintessential bohemian newlywed couple, drinking and dancing the nights away in Greenwich Village? It's Edith Head's costume design, though, that makes this film a must-see for the stylish girl. Check it out and copy whatever look you can.
COCKTAIL: Harvest Punch (page 87).

LIVE AND LET DIE 1973
Roger Moore will always be my favorite 007, but every incarnation of the dashing British Secret Service agent sets a standard for male style. A very young and stylish Jane Seymour debuts here as the tarot-reading clairvoyant "Solitaire." Watch this beautiful Bond girl in action and you might just forgive her

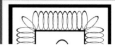

future fashion faux pas as Dr. Quinn, Medicine Woman.
COCKTAIL: The Bombed Girl (page 15).

ANNIE HALL 1977
Woody Allen's classic romantic comedy is one of his most popular films. It stars Diane Keaton as Woody's wonderfully ditzy girlfriend with a genius for the menswear look.
COCKTAIL: Sidecar (page 123).

FLASHDANCE 1983
This dancefest inspired girls everywhere to don cut-off sweatshirts and legwarmers, even if they could never come close to Jennifer Beals's moves.
COCKTAIL: Lady Rita (page 50).

PRETTY WOMAN 1990
This updated take on *My Fair Lady* established Julia Roberts as a box-office sensation. A prostitute dresses up and learns ladylike ways, but it's her spirit and integrity that win her the knight in shining armor.
COCKTAIL: Bellini (page 111).

FOUR WEDDINGS AND A FUNERAL 1994
This British rom-com stars the adorably befuddled Hugh Grant and the gorgeous Andie MacDowell as an Englishman and American woman who keep meeting up, but never at the right time. All those events provide plenty of excuses for Andie to don chic suits with huge, urbane hats.
COCKTAIL: Slopeside (page 88).

SHAKESPEARE IN LOVE 1998
This historical romantic comedy took menswear for women to a whole new level. Only Gwyneth Paltrow could look as fetching disguised as a boy as she does as a wealthy merchant's daughter who falls in love with a young Shakespeare.
COCKTAIL: The Classic (page 109).

CHOCOLAT 2000
Who isn't a fan of finding love in the midst of a confectionery spree, especially when it involves heavenly chocolate?
COCKTAIL: Coffee to Go-Go (page 116).

BRIDGET JONES'S DIARY 2001
True-blue girlfriends will identify with Bridget's hilarious attempts to find love, a satisfying career, a perfect figure and the right underwear for romantic occasions.
COCKTAIL: Fuzzy Navel (page 28).

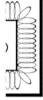

95

LEGALLY BLONDE 2001
Reese Witherspoon stars as a fashion merchandising major who applies to Harvard Law School to win back her boyfriend. She discovers she's got a knack for law but doesn't let that put an end to her fashionista ways.
COCKTAIL: Strawberry Mojito (page 73).

THE DEVIL WEARS PRADA 2006
This humorous behind-the-scenes look at the workings of a high-fashion magazine is based on a book that was loosely based on the author's hair-raising experiences working for Anna Wintour at *Vogue*.
COCKTAIL: Coco's Pearls (page 42).

SEX AND THE CITY 2008
The movie continuation of the tales of four quintessentially stylish girls.
COCKTAIL: Cosmopolitan (page 29).

wine cocktails

Sock It to Me
SERVES 4

Last New Year's Eve I brought a batch of these unusual cocktails to a party. The pineapple works as a sweet complement to the Japanese rice wine.

1 cup ice

8 oz. (237ml) sake

4 oz. (118ml) pineapple juice

4 oz. (118ml) maraschino cherry juice

8 pineapple chunks for garnish

4 picks for garnish

● Pour all liquid ingredients into a cocktail shaker filled with ice, then mix well. Pour into martini glasses, garnish with pineapple chunks on picks and serve.

Shoes
Platform heels,
for a new
perspective on the
new year!

Just Peachy

SERVES 4

These days, some people are trading the baby shower for a "Sip and See" after the baby arrives. I think this might be the way to go. You look better, feel better (well, except for being so tired you're dizzy) and you get to wear something stylish. All this while your friends fuss over your beautiful new addition.

97

Shoes
Slingbacks will get you back on your feet!

1 cup ice

4 oz. (118ml) Chambord raspberry liqueur

4 oz. (118ml) Mathilde Pêches peach liqueur

2 oz. (59ml) freshly squeezed lemon juice

1 bottle (750ml) Prosecco

● In a cocktail shaker filled with ice, mix the raspberry and peach liqueurs and the lemon juice. Strain the mixture evenly into champagne flutes. Top with Prosecco and serve.

French 75
Kir Royale

Springtime
in Paris
The Americana

The
Showstopper

champagne

Broadway
Bellissimo
The Classic

Love Hangover
The Bellini

champagne drinks

It's undeniable—there's no sexier drink on earth than a champagne cocktail. Even the tall, slender glass is sexy. So pour yourself into that slinky shift, strap on your stilettos and get ready to wow.

Champagne is the perfect celebration libation. We drink it to celebrate graduations, engagements, weddings, birthdays, new babies, new jobs, New Year's Eve. Like a new party dress, it makes any occasion feel more festive. There are, however, a lot more newsworthy moments to drink to if you think about it—a new season, a new stage, a new time in your life. And if you're nervous, that's OK—the bubbles really do help with the butterflies.

Champagne is perfect to drink with best friends, because life is too short not to celebrate them. They know us better than we know ourselves. We don't take enough time to appreciate them, and we don't give them enough champagne—shame on us. Let's fix both of these situations.

Serve champagne when you want your guests to feel special. You'll feel special, too, because champagne makes everything seem a little brighter. It must be all those bubbles. A Bellini can turn brunch into a full-blown affair. A Kir Royale can extend the lunch hour into hours. The Showstopper turns an at-home Oscar party into a red-carpet affair.

Champagne is a perfect exotic-locale drink, although it's quite delicious in Maine and Miami, in New York and LA, and everywhere in between, for that matter. Wherever you are, drinking champagne will make it feel glamorous and striking. Try a Springtime in Paris or a French 75 and you'll be transported to another time and place.

champagne is the ultimate accessory. No matter what you're wearing, it will elevate it to haute couture. If you're sipping a champagne cocktail, you have miles of style.

100

Springtime in Paris
SERVES 4

I was having a fabulous champagne cocktail in Paris, the world capital of style, a few years ago, and got a great idea for a book. Just leave it to Parisian champs to inspire one's creative pursuits. Note to self: Must try that again soon—there has to be a sequel in there somewhere.

6 oz. (177ml) black cherry juice

2 oz. (59ml) freshly squeezed lime juice

8 oz. (237ml) Tuaca liqueur

1 bottle (750ml) rosé champagne

● In a cocktail shaker, mix black cherry juice, lime juice and Tuaca. Divide equally among champagne flutes. Top with champagne and serve.

shoes
Bright-colored mules will put a spring in your step.

champagne drinks

The Americana
SERVES 4

This cocktail has been around for years, and though it combines seemingly strange bedfellows—champagne, whiskey and peaches—it's a true crowd-pleaser. It's very dry, however, so I do put out a small pitcher of peach nectar for those who are after a sweeter finish. Just peachy, no?

2 oz. (59ml) Jack Daniel's whiskey

2 teaspoons (10ml) fine sugar

2 oz. (59ml) peach nectar

1 cup ice

1 bottle (750ml) Brut champagne, chilled

4 peach slices for garnish

● Mix the whiskey, sugar and nectar in a cocktail shaker with ice. Shake well. Pour evenly into champagne flutes, then top with champagne. Add peach slices to garnish and serve.

Shoes
Peep-toe pumps with nailhead trim, for a rock-star look.

French 75

SERVES 4

shoes

French vintage is the inspiration here. Try a pair of ankle booties with fringe or ruffled trim.

Style is a combination of class and attitude, and French women just seem to ooze both. They are always somewhat chic and discreet, much like this classic cocktail, a close cousin of the martini. The lemon and sugars blend with the gin and bubbles for a simply divine citrus finish.

6 oz. (177ml) gin

4 oz. (118ml) freshly squeezed lemon juice

4 teaspoons (20ml) fine sugar

1 cup ice

1 bottle (750ml) champagne, chilled

● Mix the gin, lemon juice and sugar in a cocktail shaker with ice. Continue mixing until the sugar is dissolved. Pour evenly into champagne flutes. Top with champagne and serve.

champagne drinks

Kir Royale
SERVES 4

Champagne is the drink of kings, queens, royalty, nobility and sensibility. So be sensible and indulge like a queen with a Kir!

2 oz. (59ml) crème de cassis
1 bottle (750ml)
chilled champagne
4 orange twists

● Divide the crème de cassis evenly into champagne glasses. Top with bubbly. Garnish each with an orange twist and serve.

shoes
Very fabulous ones, perhaps with a bit of a noble air to them! Velvet mules in royal purple come to mind.

The Showstopper

SERVES 4

Lights! Cameras! Cocktails! I whipped up this creation for a very impromptu Oscar party last year. It was definitely divine and added to the Academy atmosphere. Ballots were printed from the computer, white lilies were set in crystal, and the fashion was worthy of the red carpet!

105

2 cups ice

8 oz. (237ml) St-Germain liqueur

8 oz. (237ml) tangerine juice

4 oz. (118ml) Absolut Citron vodka

Juice of 1 lime, freshly squeezed

1 bottle (750ml) champagne, chilled

● In a small pitcher filled with ice, mix together St-Germain, tangerine juice, vodka and lime juice. Mix well. Strain about 1½ oz. to fill the bottom third of each of 4 champagne flutes. Top with champagne and serve.

the original stylish girls

Let's raise a glass of bubbly and drink a toast to all the stylish girls of today and times past who have inspired us to be as fabulous as they are.

{ Coco Chanel }

Coco Chanel's commitment to elegant simplicity has made her name synonymous with Paris couture. Pearls and bouclé jackets paired with the all-American staple, blue jeans, and heels are a most modern wink to this fashion legend.

{ Katharine Hepburn }

Katharine Hepburn liberated women everywhere with her strong, confident pants-wearing style in films and real life. Every well-dressed woman needs a great pair of trousers that flow with smart style.

{ Audrey Hepburn }

Entire books have been written about Audrey Hepburn's inimitable style. Black was her color, or lack thereof, from head to toe, with cashmere sweaters, capri pants and ballet flats. She showed us that you can look polished and pulled together everyday, no matter your budget.

{ Grace Kelly }

Grace Kelly made us all believe we could grow up to be princesses. This Oscar-winning actress and world-renowned beauty also showed us how to be refined and ladylike with true white-glove style.

{ Marilyn Monroe }

In her glamorously sexy gowns, elbow-length gloves, baubles and mink stoles, Marilyn Monroe was a true red-carpet siren of style. She taught us that a little accessorizing (diamonds, anyone?) and an abundance of confidence go a long way.

{ Sophia Loren }

The fiery Italian sex symbol **Sophia Loren** still turns heads with her elegance and vitality. With her sophistication and plunging necklines she is a master of balancing sex symbol and elegant icon.

{ Jackie Kennedy Onassis }

Jackie Kennedy Onassis set the standard for White House style and for women nationwide in her chic suits, A-line dresses and pillbox hats. She was polished perfection and had the global fashion community all abuzz.

{ Diane von Furstenberg }

Diane von Furstenberg married into royalty, but was determined to have her own career. Her iconic jersey wrap dress has been a staple of women's wardrobes for three decades as a perfect day-to-night solution. She is an effortlessly glamorous jet-setter who inspires every woman on the go.

{ Madonna }

One of the most powerful women in entertainment, **Madonna** has reinvented her persona and her style constantly over an illustrious career spanning nearly three decades. They don't call her the Material Girl for nothing.

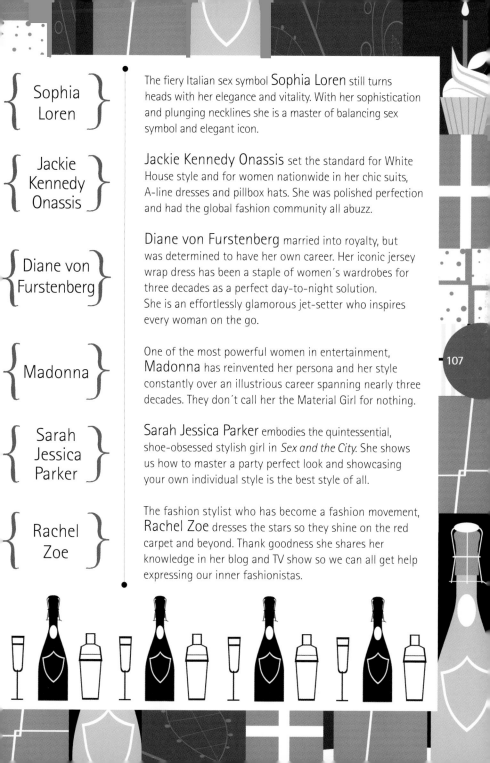

{ Sarah Jessica Parker }

Sarah Jessica Parker embodies the quintessential, shoe-obsessed stylish girl in *Sex and the City*. She shows us how to master a party perfect look and showcasing your own individual style is the best style of all.

{ Rachel Zoe }

The fashion stylist who has become a fashion movement, **Rachel Zoe** dresses the stars so they shine on the red carpet and beyond. Thank goodness she shares her knowledge in her blog and TV show so we can all get help expressing our inner fashionistas.

Broadway Bellissimo
SERVES 4

Before "the girls," as we call ourselves, saw the show *Love, Loss, and What I Wore*, we were deciding whether or not to go, and I said, "But of course we should. We are never over love, we cannot avoid loss, so...what shall we wear?" And off we went to the theater, but not before meeting up for a cocktail.

8 oz. (237ml) strawberry purée*
1 bottle (750ml) rosé champagne
4 fresh strawberries for garnish

● Pour about 2 oz. (59ml) strawberry purée into each champagne flute or enough to cover bottom third of each glass. Top with champagne. Garnish glasses with fresh strawberries using the following technique: Slice each berry two-thirds from the bottom, cutting toward the top. Place over the lip of glass. Serve.

*see recipe on page 135

Shoes
Strappy heels in a bright, Broadway-ready color.

108

The Classic
SERVES 4

Tried and true, time-tested and served
the world over, what more can you say about
the original champagne cocktail?

Small amount Angostura bitters
4 sugar cubes
2 oz. (59ml) Grand Marnier
2 oz. (59ml) brandy
1 bottle (750ml) chilled champagne
(Brut is best)
4 orange twists

● Put a few drops of bitters on each sugar
cube and place one in each champagne
flute. In a cocktail shaker or bar
glass, combine the Grand
Marnier and brandy.
Divide mixture evenly in
each glass, then top with
champagne. Garnish with
orange twists and serve.

Shoes
Mix the classic cocktail
with a touch of modern
style. Black leather
cage heels are sure to stir
things up—and sure
to add fizz.

Love Hangover
SERVES 4

Take two of these and *don't* call him in the morning!

2 oz. (59ml) passion-fruit nectar
2 oz. (59ml) pineapple juice
1 bottle (750ml) Brut champagne, chilled

● Combine the juices in a cocktail shaker or bar glass. Pour juices in champagne flutes to cover bottom third of each glass. Top with champagne and serve.

Shoes
A sexy satin slipper with a kitten heel. Add the cocktail, and you're fully dressed!

The Bellini
SERVES 4

This timeless drink, which hails from Harry´s Bar in Venice, can be served from morning to night. The purée is so easy to make, taking the ordinary cocktail from fashion exhaustion to fashion orgasm instantly.

8 oz. (237ml) white peach purée*
or peach nectar
1 bottle (750ml) Brut champagne, chilled
4 mint sprigs for garnish

● Pour the purée or nectar evenly among four champagne flutes. Slowly top with champagne. Add a mint sprig to each glass for garnish and serve.

*see recipe on page 135

eclectic cocktails & faux-fabulous mocktails

Manhattan
Pisco Sour
Pineapple
Bomb

Mint Julep
Coffee to Go-Go
Pimm's Cup

The Stiletto
Between the
Sheets

Sidecar
Passion for
Fashion

Raspberry
Faux-jito
Raspberry Lime
Rickey

The Knockoff
Lavender
Lemonade

Green Apple
Sparkler

eclectic cocktails & faux-fabulous mocktails

Oh, the sample sale—is there anything better? Designer duds at a fraction of the original price—and when people ask where you got that incredible dress or those amazing shoes, it's up to you to decide whether or not to tell them.

Just like at a sample sale, you don't know what you're going to find in this chapter. You've stocked up on the basics—vodka cocktails, gin drinks, champagne cocktails—but your wardrobe is just not complete.

Bourbon, whiskey, Kahlúa, vermouth, brandy, cognac, Southern Comfort...the possibilities are endless. I mean, a stylish girl like you must know how to make a Mint Julep, mix a Manhattan and stir things up with a batch of Pisco Sours.

Finally, we end the chapter with a selection of "mocktails"—delicious drinks with all the flavor, zip and pizzazz and none of the alcohol. Maybe you're watching your figure or nursing a cold (or a little one). Or perhaps you've volunteered to be the designated driver or cab hailer. Whatever your reason for abstaining, you'll find plenty of mixes that are so delightfully refreshing you'll never miss a thing.

So let's get started. Remember, there are no returns!

cheers! Like a few trendy new clothing items, some additions to your cocktail bar will yield dozens of options.

Mint Julep
SERVES 4

Also known as the Run for the Roses, the Kentucky Derby is the most exciting two minutes in sports and is also the start of the summer social season. You don't have to be in Kentucky to enjoy it. My friends Bets and Rod throw the best derby party every year, serving herb biscuits, cheesy potatoes and juleps galore.

2 oz. (59ml) mint-infused simple syrup*

8 oz. (237ml) bourbon

2 cups crushed ice

4 oz. (119ml) seltzer to top

8 mint leaves for garnish

shoes
Clip a few rose blooms on your shoes to complement your wide-brimmed hat and party frock.

● Combine simple syrup and bourbon in a cocktail shaker. Fill julep glasses with crushed ice and divide mixture evenly among glasses. Top with seltzer, garnish with fresh mint leaves and serve.

*see recipe on page 134

eclectic cocktails

Coffee to Go-Go
SERVES 4

We all need a little something hot and spicy once in a while, and this coffee cocktail does the trick. Rich and creamy, it's an ideal chilly-afternoon pick-me-up. Try serving it as dessert at your next dinner party.

8 oz. (237ml) espresso

4 oz. (118ml) light cream

4 oz. (118ml) Absolut Vanilia vodka

4 oz. (118ml) Kahlúa

8 oz. (237ml) heavy cream for whipping

¼ cup (59ml) grated semisweet chocolate

4 cinnamon sticks for garnish

● Prepare espresso. In a small bowl, heat cream in microwave oven on low for 30 seconds until warm. Pour espresso evenly into Irish coffee glasses and follow with light cream. Next, add vodka and Kahlúa. In another small bowl, whip the heavy cream until soft peaks form. Top off each glass with a heaping spoonful of whipped cream. Garnish with sprinklings of grated chocolate shavings and cinnamon sticks.

shoes
Soft natural-toned pumps for day; jewel tones for après dinner.

Pimm's Cup
SERVES 4

This traditional English summertime drink with deep complex flavors is perfect for tennis parties, cricket, croquet, polo matches or any backyard happening. An old British standard, Pimm's is a gin-based product made with aromatic herbs that is becoming popular stateside. Whip up a batch of these and you'll be stylish and sophisticato!

3 cups ice

8 oz. (237ml) Pimm's No. 1 Cup

4 oz. (118ml) ginger ale

4 oz. (118ml) lemon- or lime-flavored seltzer

8 maraschino cherries for garnish

Shoes
Canvas wedges are both sexy and smart for lawn games.

● Fill highball glasses with ice. Pour Pimm's evenly among glasses. Do the same with the ginger ale and seltzer. Garnish with 2 cherries per glass and serve.

eclectic cocktails

Manhattan
SERVES 4

I'll take Manhattan, and then Brooklyn! This classic cocktail is a must-have for your recipe repertoire, whether you live in the Big Apple or the Big Easy.

1 cup ice
4 dashes Angostura bitters
6 oz. (177ml) rye whiskey
2 oz. (59ml) sweet vermouth
4 maraschino cherries for garnish

shoes
Ultrafeminine black strappy heels.

● In a cocktail shaker filled with ice, add the bitters, whiskey and vermouth. Shake well. Strain mixture into rocks or lowball glasses. Garnish with cherries and serve.

Pisco Sour
SERVES 4

Break out the passport and head off to South America! Pisco is a Chilean variety of brandy made from white Muscat grapes that possesses a floral essence—just the right go-to girls' cocktail. Put on some Gypsy Kings and get shaking.

8 oz. (237ml) Pisco ABA

3 teaspoons (15ml) key lime juice

2 tablespoons (30ml) superfine sugar

1 egg white

3 cups ice—1 for the shaker, 2 for the glasses

● Mix all ingredients in a cocktail shaker filled with ice. Shake until frothy. Strain into ice-filled rocks glasses. Serve immediately.

shoes
Dancing shoes, of course—*jay, caramba!*

eclectic cocktails

Pineapple Bomb
SERVES 4

These mini cocktails hit the spot.
The perfect aperitif pre-party or before
bar-hopping, they are a fantastic start
to a fun-filled evening.

4 oz. (118ml) Southern Comfort
2 oz. (59ml) triple sec
2 oz. (59ml) pineapple juice
1 cup ice
2 oz. (59ml) Fresca soda

● Mix all ingredients except Fresca in a
cocktail shaker with ice. Add Fresca, pour
evenly into mini glasses and serve.

shoes
Gold satin pumps
will light up
the night.

The Stiletto
SERVES 4

This cocktail came about at a gathering at a friend's house. She had a small pitcher of hibiscus reduction in the fridge, which she had been adding to seltzer on a daily basis. Naturally, I said we should try it in a cocktail. My friend agreed that the spiked version is even better than the original.

2 cups ice
2 oz. (59ml) gin
6 oz. (178ml) lillet
3 oz. (89ml) hibiscus reduction*
2 oz. (59ml) lemon juice
4 oz. (118ml) seltzer

Shoes
Hibiscus-hued
stilettos...in case
you couldn't
guess.

● In a cocktail shaker filled halfway with ice, pour the first four ingredients. Mix well. Add seltzer, strain into martini glasses and serve.

*see recipe on page 134

eclectic cocktails

Between the Sheets
SERVES 4

Who says a stylish girl can't be a little bit naughty? Mix up a batch of this smooth-as-silk concoction and see if it stirs up a romantic moment or two....

8 oz. (237ml) brandy
4 oz. (118ml) Bacardi light rum
2 oz. (59ml) clear Curaçao
2 oz. (59ml) freshly squeezed lemon juice
1 cup ice

● Pour all ingredients into a cocktail shaker filled with ice. Shake well, strain into red wine goblets and serve.

shoes
Mules are easy to slip on...and slip off.

Sidecar
SERVES 4

The stylish girl is always up on the hottest trends, including television shows. This cocktail is a 1960s classic that is making its way into shows and movies set in the period. Although traditional sour mix is usually called for, the contemporary stylish girl can use a mix of fresh juices and a touch of sugar to sweeten things up a notch.

1 cup ice
8 oz. (237ml) Cognac
4 oz. (118ml) Cointreau
2 oz. (59ml) Stylish Girl's Sour Mix*
4 lemon twists for garnish

● In a cocktail shaker filled with ice, vigorously mix all ingredients together. Strain mixture evenly into rocks glasses. Garnish with lemon twists and serve.

*see recipe on page 135

One decade at a time

Just as fashions change through the years, so do cocktail trends! Here's a quick look at the past decades, the fashion styles that defined them and the cocktails that made the perfect accessories.

1940s

● The Forties found women getting out of the kitchen and into the workforce, many earning their first paychecks and spending them at the new department stores. Money was tight, but girls had a patriotic duty to shop for Hollywood-inspired dresses—the broader the shoulders the better. With the Big Band sound on the radio, cocktails were flowing and Tom Collins was the drink of choice. I've updated it as the **Tina Collins** (page 45) as a salute to these Forties femmes.

1950s

● In the fab Fifties, full skirts with yards and yards of fabric rocked the scene, and heels and gloves were de rigueur for hitting the town. The bar was always hopping, happy days were here again and rock 'n' roll was here to stay. The daily cocktail took center stage, including the very fashionable **Mai Tai** (page 78).

1960s

● Office culture ruled this "mad" decade with smokes, witty banter and cocktails—from the infamous three-martini lunch meetings to working dinners. Sleeveless sheaths, sweater sets and pillbox hats in ode to Jackie were all the rage. But no party was complete without a home bar to mix up a batch of **Gibson Martinis** (page 35).

1970s

● Peace, love and sex flourished in the decade of disco. In the swinging Seventies bold geometrics, hippie prints and micro miniskirts flooded the scene. And the communal punch bowl shared grooviness all around, doling out servings of **Tequila Sunrise** (page 60). Mix it up and feel the love!

1980s

● Wall Street ruled the Eighties with "Greed Is Good" as its mantra. The excesses of the decade brought nonstop good times on the road to the top. Madonna wannabes and corporate climbers rubbed shoulders with Valley Girls and preppies. Brands were all important, and your cocktail of choice was carefully scrutinized, too. The conspicuous consumption of **Fuzzy Navels** (page 28) was the height of fashion.

125

1990s

● Grunge, flannel, punk, goth, preppy, sporty, neon, the Nineties had it all. It proved to be a melting pot of fashion as we counted down to Y2K and the end of a millennium. Cocktails followed fashion, with mixology taking off. Tequila was the big buzz, and the **Margarita** (page 56) had its coming-out party. Anything goes when you're drinking with *Friends!*

2000s

● Today's fashion and cocktails are globally inspired. After all, it's always 5 o'clock somewhere. Instant communication has made us a one-world family. We blog, we text, we tweet, we live instantly. The home bar is the hub for entertaining, and the global fave of the moment is the **Mojito** (pages 73–75). While we sip, we're thinking of acting responsibly, giving back, saving the planet and always looking to the future.

faux-fabulous mocktails

Passion for Fashion
SERVES 4

Whatever style is your passion, this fruity festival of a cocktail will complement it. You'll be refreshed and runway-ready after sipping this delightful concoction.

12 oz. (355ml) Goya passion-fruit nectar

8 oz. (237ml) pineapple juice

2 oz. (59ml) freshly squeezed lemon juice

8 oz. (237ml) sparkling water

3 cups ice

4 lemon slices for garnish

shoes
Strut your stuff in ankle booties.

• In a small pitcher, mix together the nectar, pineapple juice and lemon juice. Add the seltzer and pour into ice-filled highball glasses. Garnish with lemon slices and serve.

Be the perfect hostess by mixing up some sensational "mocktails" for teetotalling friends. The next several pages of delicious, alcohol-free recipes give you lots of options.

Raspberry Faux-jito
SERVES 4

Leaving out the rum doesn't make this concoction any less delectable. And you'll be steady on your feet while you dance the night away.

12 mint leaves, plus more for garnish

1 lime, sliced into wedges

1 cup fresh raspberries

1 teaspoon (5ml) superfine sugar

8 oz. (237ml) lemon-lime soda
(Sprite, Fresca, etc.)

2 cups ice

8 oz. (237ml) lime-flavored seltzer

● In a small pitcher or cocktail shaker, muddle 12 mint leaves, lime wedges, raspberries and sugar. Add soda and divide mixture evenly into ice-filled rocks glasses. Top with seltzer, garnish with additional mint leaves and serve.

Shoes
Bright red heels with ankle straps to keep them on your dancing feet.

faux-fabulous mocktails

Raspberry Lime Rickey
SERVES 4

There are many variations on the lime rickey—some with alcohol, some without. This zero-proof version gets an extra burst of flavor thanks to the addition of raspberry syrup.

8 oz. (237ml) limeade

4 oz. (118ml) raspberry syrup

8 lime slices, plus 4 for garnish (about 2 limes)

2 cups ice

16 oz. (473ml) sparkling water

shoes
You'll be quick on your feet in Vans slip-ons—you choose the color.

● In a cocktail shaker, mix together the limeade and raspberry syrup. Place 2 slices of lime in the bottom of each of 4 rocks glasses, then add ice. Pour shaker ingredients evenly into the glasses. Top with sparkling water. Garnish with lime slices and serve.

Shoes
Festive, low-heeled slides are ideal for mingling at the soiree.

The Knockoff
SERVES 4

Fruity sweetness marries delightfully with ginger-ale bubbles for thirst-quenching perfection. I serve this at many gatherings and no one even notices it's a fake.

4 oz. (118ml) cranberry juice
8 oz. (237ml) white grape juice
4 oz. (118ml) grenadine
16 oz. (473ml) ginger ale
3 cups ice
4 lemon slices for garnish

● In a small pitcher, mix together the two juices and the grenadine. Add ginger ale, then pour mixture into ice-filled Collins glasses. Garnish with lemon slices and serve.

129

faux-fabulous mocktails

Lavender Lemonade
SERVES 4

This aromatic lemonade is so delicious, no one will miss the alcohol.

5 lavender petals, plus additional blossoms for garnish

8 oz. (237ml) water

4 teaspoons (20ml) superfine sugar

3 cups ice

8 oz. (237ml) pomegranate juice

1 24-oz. (710ml) bottle Lorina sparkling pink lemonade

shoes
Lavender-hued pumps.

● Place lavender petals, water and sugar in a small saucepan. Bring to a boil then simmer until reduced by half, stirring occasionally. Strain mixture into a small bowl, then chill for at least one hour. Fill a large pitcher with ice, then add sugar mix, pomegranate juice and sparkling lemonade. Pour into Collins glasses, garnish with lavender blossoms and serve.

Green Apple Sparkler
SERVES 4

Pucker up! Fresh green apple juice (available at most markets) combined with lemonade makes for a tartly refreshing cocktail. It's perfect for backyard barbecues or picnics in the park.

16 oz. (473ml) fresh green apple juice
8 oz. (237ml) lemonade
3 cups ice
8 oz. (237ml) lemon-flavored seltzer
4 lemon slices for garnish

● In a cocktail shaker, mix together apple juice and lemonade. Pour into ice-filled Collins glasses. Top with seltzer, garnish with lemon slices and serve.

Shoes
Moccasins are back in style and are oh-so-comfy for outdoor fun.

accessories

basic recipes

Simple Syrup

Simple syrup is a key ingredient in many cocktail recipes, as a liquid sweetener that incorporates easily.

MAKES SCANT 1 CUP

1 cup (237ml) water

1 cup (237ml) sugar

● Combine water and sugar in a medium saucepan and bring to a boil. Stir constantly until the sugar has dissolved and the liquid is clear, about 5 minutes. Remove from the heat and let cool. The syrup will keep, refrigerated in an airtight container, for up to one week.

134

where to shop

Crate&Barrel
crate&barrel.com

Williams-Sonoma
williams-sonoma.com

HomeGoods
homegoods.com

Mint-Infused Simple Syrup

(for Mint Julep, page 115)

A variation on basic simple syrup, that is a must for a successful Mint Julep.

MAKES SCANT 1 CUP

1 cup (237ml) water

1 cup (237ml) sugar

1 cup (237ml) mint leaves, washed

● Combine water and sugar in a saucepan. Bring to a boil, stirring constantly until sugar dissolves and the liquid becomes clear— about 5 minutes. Remove from heat and add washed mint leaves. Let mixture sit for 15 minutes. Strain the syrup and discard the mint leaves. The syrup will keep in the refrigerator in an airtight container for up to 2 weeks.

Hibiscus Reduction

(for The Stiletto, page 121)

Flowers aren't just for arranging. They can also make beautifully aromatic cocktail mix-ins.

MAKES SCANT 2 CUPS

2 cups (473ml) water

2 cups (473ml) sugar

1 cup (237ml) dried hibiscus flowers

● Combine water, sugar and flowers in a medium-size saucepan and bring to a boil. Boil until sugar is dissolved. Strain into pitcher. Reduction will keep in the refrigerator for up to 2 weeks.

Stylish Girl's Sour Mix
(for Sidecar, page 123)

You can make sour mix with lemon juice or lime juice, but I like to use both for maximum flavor.

MAKES 4 OZ. (118ML)

2 oz. (59ml) freshly squeezed lemon juice

2 oz. (59ml) freshly squeezed lime juice

1 teaspoon (5ml) super fine sugar

● In a tall glass, mix together juices and sugar. Stir until sugar has dissolved. Sour mix will keep refrigerated in an airtight container for up to 2 weeks.

White Peach Puree
(for Bellini, page 111)

Making your own puree will put your Bellini over the top.

MAKES 2 CUPS

6 white peaches

2 teaspoons (10ml) sugar

● Add peaches to medium-size saucepan filled halfway with water and bring to boil. Boil for 2 minutes. Remove from heat and let cool a bit. Peel peaches while still warm. Cut into chunks, discarding pits. Place peaches and sugar in a blender or food processor and puree until smooth. Pour into a pitcher and chill before serving. Will keep in refrigerator for 1 week.

Strawberry Puree
(for Broadway Bellissimo, page 108)

Fresh strawberries and raspberry-flavored vodka mingle in this recipe for a deliciously fruity mixer.

MAKES APPROX. 3 CUPS

4 cups (1 quart) fresh strawberries

4 oz. (118ml) Absolut Raspberri vodka

● Wash and cut fresh strawberries into small chunks or slices. Soak them in vodka for up to 1 hour. Once soaked, place in a blender and puree until smooth, about 1 minute. The puree will keep in the refrigerator in an airtight container for 1 week.

cocktail bar lingo

These "bon mots" will help you sound as good as you look.

Bar spoon A teaspoon with an extra-long handle; perfect to stir a drink from top to bottom, even in the largest pitcher.

Bitters A bittersweet alcoholic beverage made of roots, herbs and other plants that is often added to cocktails as a flavoring agent. It can also be served as a digestif.

Chambord A French black raspberry liqueur made from berries, vanilla, citrus, honey and cognac. With a long history dating back to Louis XIV, a rich color, and an intense sweetness, it adds an elegant touch to a mixed drink.

Champagne flute A wine glass with a stem and long, narrow bowl. The small opening slows the escape of air from champagne, keeping your bubbly bubbling longer.

Cocktail picks A fancy little toothpick used to skewer olives, onions or fruit placed in drinks. A nice pick will make your drink look extra classy, and your fingers can stay dry even if you decide to nibble on the garnish before your drink is done.

Cocktail shaker A two- or three-piece accessory used to shake mixed drinks without spilling, strain them if necessary and pour them with ease. You can improvise with two different-size glasses—meaning there's no reason not to shake what you've got.

Collins glass A glass with no stem; like a highball glass but narrower and taller.

Garnish Any decorative element added to a cocktail, such as fruit, olives, herbs, coffee beans, flowers or chocolate shavings. Often a drink will use a combination of two or more garnishes.

Highball glass Your basic glass: no stem, no handle, no muss, no fuss. It's shorter than a Collins glass and taller than a lowball glass.

Hurricane glass A curvy glass with a squat stem, often used for frozen drinks. It gets its name from its classic hurricane-lamp shape.

Limoncello A sweet Italian lemon liqueur usually from Southern Italy. Made of lemon zest, alcohol, water and sugar, it is a lovely lemon yellow and is delicious on its own or mixed in a cocktail.

Liqueur An alcoholic beverage that has been flavored with fruit, herbs, nuts, spices, flowers or cream and bottled with added sugar. Liqueurs are typically quite sweet.

Lowball glass The little cousin of the highball glass. It's also known as an old fashioned glass.

Margarita glass A glass with a stem and wide bowl that comes in a variety of sizes. Also a great way to serve cocktail-party fare like shrimp or dip.

Marry To let ingredients sit for a little while. Sometimes you have to give them time to mingle to allow the flavors to combine well.

Martini glass A stemmed glass with a bowl shaped like an upside-down cone.

Mini glass / Shot glass A small glass that holds one measure (or "jigger") of liquor, which can be used to mix a drink or sipped directly from the glass—or, of course, taken as a shot! Makes a fun souvenir, too.

Muddle To crush fruit and/or herbs in the bottom of a tall glass with a wooden pestle or "muddler" to release their juices and flavors in a concentrated fashion.

Muddler A pestle-like tool with a heavy end used to crush fruits or herbs at the bottom of a glass.

Parfait amour Parfait amour is a liqueur. A vibrant shade of purple, it is often used in cocktails primarily for its color and is generally created from a Curaçao liqueur base. It's flavored with rose petals, vanilla and almonds.

Pitcher Any large container with a spout and handle; the perfect place to mix cocktails for large groups.

Prosecco A sparkling white wine similar to champagne.

Reduce To use a cooking technique that decreases the volume and concentrates the flavor of a liquid by boiling it. The result is a "reduction."

Rim To adhere sugar or salt to the edge of a glass for extra taste and visual oomph; done before pouring the cocktail into the glass. Place sugar or salt on a plate, wet the rim of your glass (with a lemon, a lime or a little of your drink), and simply place the glass upside-down on the plate. When you pull it away you'll have a perfectly rimmed glass.

Rocks glass A.K.A. lowball glass or old fashioned glass. Just the right size for your cocktail on the rocks.

Shake A quick and effective way to make sure your mixed drink is good and mixed. To do: Place all of the ingredients in the shaker and fill with ice to just below the rim. Put the top on tightly and shake with sass and style. About twenty seconds is good—if you overshake, you will dilute the cocktail.

Skewers A thin bit of metal or wood that can pierce and hold food. It's a good way to keep your olives from floating to the top of your martini.

Splash A small amount.

Sprigs Small bits of herbs that are often used as a garnish.

Strain After a drink has been mixed, straining is often required to discard any bits of fruit or seeds, etc. Most cocktail shakers come with a strainer. If yours does not, any mesh strainer will do.

Swizzle sticks Fancy name for a stirrer, the swizzle stick is sometimes made from sugar or honey. It has a dual purpose: adding sweetness to the drink as it dissolves, while mixing bits of herbs or fruit that may have settled to the bottom of the glass.

Top To fill up the rest of the space in the glass, often with seltzer (as in "seltzer to top").

Twists Little pieces of citrus peel, often spiraled in a helix shape, used to garnish or add flavor to a drink.

Wine glass Stemware designed for wine; typically, goblets for red wine are rounder.

downloadable playlist

Songs for every occasion, every outfit, every cocktail.

dance party

SONG	ARTIST	ALBUM
"Lay All Your Love on Me"	ABBA	*ABBA Gold*
"Boom Boom Pow"	Black Eyed Peas	*The E.N.D.*
"Love Drunk"	Boys Like Girls	*Love Drunk*
"Vogue"	Madonna	*Celebration*
"Evacuate the Dancefloor"	Cascada	*Evacuate the Dancefloor*
"Right Round"	Flo Rida	*Right Round*
"So What"	P!nk	*Funhouse*
"Disturbia"	Rihanna	*Good Girl Gone Bad*

dinner party

SONG	ARTIST	ALBUM
"Daughters"	John Mayer	*Heavier Things*
"Paparazzi"	Lady Gaga	*The Fame*
"Fallen"	Lauren Wood	*Cat Trick*
"Maria Maria"	Santana	*Supernatural*
"Desert Rose"	Sting	*Brand New Day*
"Sway"	Michael Bublé	*Michael Bublé*
"Someday"	John Legend	*August Rush (Music from the Motion Picture)*

pool party

SONG	ARTIST	ALBUM
"I Wanna"	All-American Rejects	*When the World Comes Down*
"Anyone Else but You"	The Moldy Peaches	*Moldy Peaches*
"Come Away With Me"	Norah Jones	*Come Away With Me*
"California Girls"	The Beach Boys	*Sounds of Summer*
"Little Miss Can't Be Wrong"	The Spin Doctors	*Pocket Full of Kryptonite*
"Brown Eyed Girl"	Van Morrison	*Van Morrison*
"Say Hey (I Love You)	Michael Franti & Spearhead	*All Rebel Rockers*
"Beautiful Day"	U2	*All That You Can't Leave Behind*

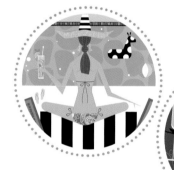

Go to apple.com/itunes to download this list of tunes that will take you from poolside to the dance floor and everywhere in between.

girls' night in

SONG	ARTIST	ALBUM
"Girls Just Want to Have Fun"	Cyndi Lauper	*Cyndi Lauper: Collections*
"Single Ladies (Put a Ring on It)"	Beyoncé	*I Am...Sasha Fierce*
"Material Girl"	Madonna	*Celebration*
"Red Red Wine"	UB40	*The Very Best of UB40*
"Goodbye Girl"	Squeeze	*Squeeze: Gold*
"These Are Days"	10,000 Maniacs	*Our Time in Eden*
"Bubbly"	Colbie Caillat	*Coco*
"Our Lips Are Sealed"	The Go-Go's	*Return to the Valley of the Go-Go's*

Acknowledgments

● A book comes together much like a stylish outfit: There are separate pieces that when put together well make a fashion statement. I would like to thank everyone who helped to create this ensemble: my editors, Michelle Bredeson and Wendy Williams—without their support and gentle deadline reminders, this stylish girl would have been fashionably late—and art director Diane Lamphron and illustrator Bee, who brought the stylish girl to life and gave her great accessories to boot! And many thanks to Trisha Malcolm, who inspires me to always be stylish.

This book is dedicated to my "core four." A friend makes you a better person from the inside, allowing your true style to show.

index

141

142